# LOS ANGELES
## By Stroller

Ted and Jennifer Hong
2242 Bentley Avenue #1
Los Angeles, CA 90064

A CITY BY STROLLER GUIDE

# LOS ANGELES
## By Stroller

Shelley-Anne Wooderson

CUMBERLAND HOUSE
NASHVILLE, TENNESSEE

LOS ANGELES BY STROLLER
PUBLISHED BY CUMBERLAND HOUSE PUBLISHING, INC.
431 Harding Industrial Drive
Nashville, TN 37211

Cover design: James Duncan Creative
Book design: Mary Sanford

**Library of Congress Cataloging-in-Publication Data**
Wooderson, Shelley Anne.
  Los Angeles by stroller / Shelley Anne Wooderson.
     p. cm.
  Includes index.
  ISBN 1-58182-451-3 (pbk. : alk. paper)
  1. Los Angeles (Calif.)—Guidebooks. 2. Family recreation—California—
Los Angeles—Guidebooks. 3. Preschool children—Travel—California—Los Angeles—
Guidebooks. 4. Parents—Travel—California—Los Angeles—Guidebooks. I. Title.
  F869.L83W66 2005
  917.94'9404'54—dc22

                                                                    2005006503

Printed in the United States of America
1 2 3 4 5 6 7—10 09 08 07 06 05

This book is for Julie and Katherine,
without whom I would never have needed a stroller.
Thank you both for enriching my life.

Ted and Jennifer Hong
2242 Bentley Avenue #1
Los Angeles, CA 90064

Ted and Jennifer Hong
2242 Bentley Avenue #1
Los Angeles, CA 90064

# Contents

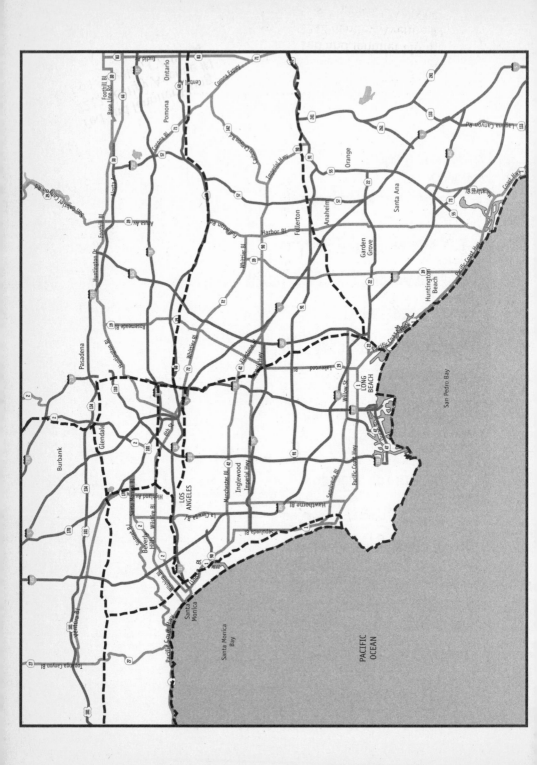

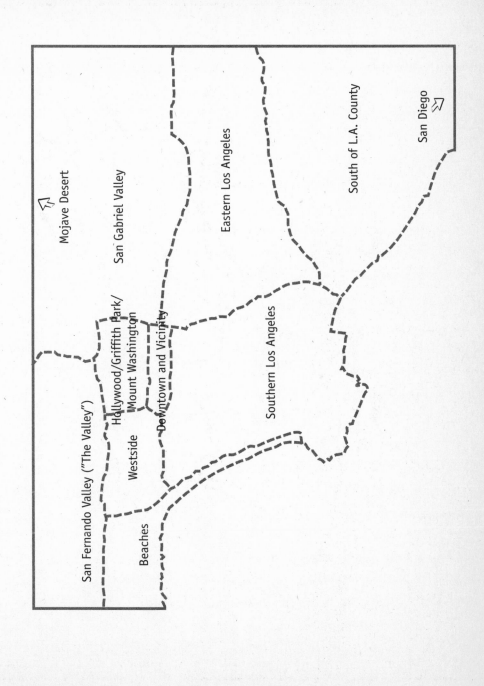

Mojave Desert

San Gabriel Valley

Eastern Los Angeles

South of L.A. County

San Diego

San Fernando Valley ("The Valley")

Hollywood/Griffith Park/
Mount Washington

Westside

Downtown and Vicinity

Southern Los Angeles

Beaches

# Introduction

Without my intense dislike for housework, this book never would have been written. I find it easier to take my kids out exploring than to stay home and clean up after them. Having two kids almost four years apart has kept me pushing a stroller around Los Angeles for what seems like millennia.

As I started to explore with my kids, I was amazed at how places I once loved as a teenager, or even as an adult, offered a completely different experience to me as a mother. This book does not tell you what the best places in L.A. are, but I hope it tells you the best places in L.A. to take preschool age children.

I've tried to cover the basics, focusing on Los Angeles County. Any venues outside of L.A. County were added because they are popular attractions that residents would drive to.

Is what I say about each place true? Well, for me it is. If I met vile, obnoxious guards or helpful, caring guides, this definitely colored my view. I am opinionated; you may not agree with my take on a venue, but I hope my observations and experiences will help you take your kids out into the world better prepared for the adventure.

There are so many venues in Los Angeles, so much more to do, so much more culture than I could ever imagine. I see people spending immense amounts of money to go to amusement parks when there are venues that cost much less and are closer to home—yet we often don't know about them. We were on our way to an amusement park one day, and my oldest (five at the time) said, "Mommy, another amusement park, do we have to? Can't we go to a museum?" So don't be reluctant to expose your kids to museums and art galleries; they just may love them, especially if you know which ones are best to take them to.

Now: a short discussion of the method to my madness. The ratings system is based on how I feel about the place. I'm sure my children wouldn't agree with my ratings, but they never factor the cost of an outing into its worth. I have put a note as to how many adults I think the trip requires. If you are taking more than one child, this is a useful guide. In my experience there are just some places (like amusement parks) that are sheer torture if you attempt them alone with multiple children. If you see a place listed in bold print within another venue, then it is written up separately elsewhere in the book. And, as always, opening hours and prices can and will change—and may already have done so.

I hope this book encourages you to go out and start your own explorations.

May the tour guides be understanding, the security guards be kind, and the restrooms always be equipped with changing tables.

## A Guide to the Ratings in This Book

| | |
|---|---|
| 🚼🚼🚼🚼🚼 | This place is great and inexpensive, so go already. |
| 🚼🚼🚼🚼 | Definitely fun, not perfect, but what is? |
| 🚼🚼🚼 | Still worth the trip. |
| 🚼🚼 | Beats going stir-crazy at home . . . maybe. |
| 🚼 | For masochists only. |
| 0 strollers | What were you thinking!? |

# LOS ANGELES
## By Stroller

# Downtown and Vicinity

# Air and Space Gallery

Located in Exposition Park, the Air and Space Gallery is technically part of the **California Science Center**, but it's sort of the Science Center's neglected little sister and an outing all by itself.

Even finding the Air and Space Gallery can be a challenge because half the signs don't list it, but just look for a tall building with a plane stuck on the side. Once inside the four-story structure, you'll see planes hanging from the ceiling. The entire building is built like a warehouse with three mezzanine levels. This works great for the exhibits, which often cover more than one floor, but I would recommend staying away from this place if you or your children have a fear of heights. Due to the layout it can also be challenging chasing your toddlers up and down metal staircases. There is an elevator—one of the largest I've ever seen—but who wants to ride when they can fly down the stairs with Mommy screaming at them the whole way?

The highlights for the younger crowd include a helicopter they can "fly" and parachutes they can launch from the ceiling. (Go to the ground floor for another fun view of the parachutes.)

The Discovery Center, which would have been great, was closed. The staff told me it closed two years ago due to budget cuts but should be open again soon. The rest of the gallery showed signs of cutbacks; for example, the store on the second floor where you enter

**RATING**

**ADDRESS/PHONE/WEB SITE**
700 State Drive
Los Angeles 90037
323-SCIENCE

**HOURS**
Mon–Fri, 10:00 a.m.–1:00 p.m.; Sat–Sun, 1:00 p.m.–4:00 p.m.; Closed New Year's Day, Thanksgiving, and Christmas

**COST**
Free

**PARKING**
$6

**STROLLER ACCESS**
Great for up to a double-wide stroller

**MORE THAN ONE ADULT NEEDED?**
No

**THE LOWDOWN**
If you go here first and you still have some time left, go to the main California Science Center.

was devoid of merchandise, and several of the exhibits were broken on the day we went. But it was still worth a visit. When you are on your way out, let your kids run out any energy they have left after the stairs. There is a beautiful rose garden to get lost in before you go home.

## rnia Science Center

California Science Center is one of those places that you will have to come back to time and time again just to see everything—the great news is, it's free! Here is an amazing offering of hands-on, visually graphic, incredibly entertaining science.

This place might even make you wonder if maybe you should've have pursued chemistry or physics longer, instead of giving it up as soon as you could. Or maybe that's just me. The Science Center explores the physical world around us, from how houses are built to withstand earthquakes (if they wait for a turn, your kids can stand in a room that simulates an earthquake; they can also build a freestanding arch out of large, soft blocks) to how our own bodies work.

The Discovery Room (on the third floor, in the Creative World

**RATING**

🪑🪑🪑🪑🪑

**ADDRESS/PHONE/WEB SITE**

700 State Drive
Los Angeles 90037
323-724-3623
www.californiasciencecenter.org

**HOURS**

Every day, 10:00 a.m.–5:00 p.m.; Closed New Year's Day, Thanksgiving, and Christmas

**COST**

Free, although donations of $5 for adults are requested; the IMAX theater is $7.50 for adults and $4.50 for children

**PARKING**

$6

**STROLLER ACCESS**

Adequate for up to a double-wide stroller

**MORE THAN ONE ADULT NEEDED?**

No

**THE LOWDOWN**

This place can be crowded, particularly on rainy weekends and weekday mornings, and although there are on-site restaurants, there can be long waits for food.

area) is set up especially for young kids to build and pretend and play, although it can be rather crowded, and you may have to wait to enter.

In the World of Life (on the second floor), you will find another Discovery Room that is usually less crowded. There your kids can play with puzzles or look at real snakes, frogs, or hissing cockroaches. This area also features Tess, the BodyWorks dummy. This fifty-foot woman moves and appears to talk while she demonstrates how the human body works. I've taken five kids through this display and only the seven-year-old, the oldest, was scared and refused to stay; the rest enjoyed it. You can peek inside before the show begins, and ask your kids if it will scare them if the big, pretend lady opens her eyes and talks—they'll know.

The **Air and Space Gallery** is another part of the Science Center. There is also an IMAX theater, the only part of the museum that isn't free. If you want to watch a big-screen movie, go for it. Nothing against IMAX, but I'd rather run around after my kids while they play with small tornado-making machines or try to make white light turn into a rainbow—they have enough time to sit and watch movies at home.

# Chinatown

Chinatown is my favorite place for a meal out with the kids. The food is great, restaurants are reasonably priced, and when your kids get bored, they can spend time feeding the goldfish in the outdoor ponds. Then, when you have finished eating, you can wander through countless small stores with odd and inexpensive trinkets, all of which your kids will want right now. It's fun for adults and kids, because most of the shops are child-friendly; and if they aren't, leave—there's always another vendor willing to be nice.

My favorite way to get to Chinatown is to take the train. However, there *is* parking available for a price. Chinatown hosts many festivals throughout the year, the biggest of which is, of course, Chinese New Year. I took my kids to it and they loved it. Be forewarned: if your kids are afraid of loud noises, consider ear plugs—or stay away—as millions of small firecrackers will be going off. The fireworks are not the kind you see on the Fourth of July, but rather small "double happy" bangers whose sole purpose is to make noise. Several hundred are tied together and lit. The air fills with smoke and staccato gunfire-type noise, the kind that would have sent me screaming to my mom when I was a kid. But if your kids can tolerate the noise, buy them some

**RATING**

**ADDRESS/PHONE/WEB SITE**
Between Hill and Spring Streets
Cesar Chavez and the Pasadena Freeway
www.chinatownla.com

**COST**
Free

**PARKING**
Approx. $6 unless you take the Metro

**HOURS**
Many of the restaurants are closed on Mondays, and the weekend is definitely the most fun when the most vendors are open.

**STROLLER ACCESS**
Adequate, but the shops are usually packed so be prepared to leave the stroller outside and carry the younger kids

**MORE THAN ONE ADULT NEEDED?**
No

**THE LOWDOWN**
If you like Chinese food you will love it. The Metro Gold Line is the best way to get there. Fireworks and noisemakers are a major feature of the New Year's parade; keep that in mind when you go.

little poppers that crack when they hit the ground, and let them be a part of the experience.

My four-year-old stood for two hours in the freezing cold, completely transfixed, as lion dancers, martial artists, dragons, and floats went by. This parade is very long, so take some snacks or, alternatively, find a restaurant with a view on the parade route where you can sit to enjoy at least part of the procession. The parade comes north on Broadway and then turns and goes south on Hill, so you can actually see it twice if you cross streets. However, my recommendation is to find a restaurant on Hill and spend at least part of the parade time inside. Then go out and watch the spectacle on Hill. People don't realize how long the route is, so by the time the parade gets to Hill, much of the crowd has thinned out and gone home. To get there, take the Gold Line Metro train, arrive a little late, and go up to Hill Street.

Take your kids to Chinatown any time (save the fortune cookies for feeding to the overweight goldfish), and if your kids don't mind noise, catch the Chinese New Year celebrations.

# Dodgers Stadium/Elysian Park

Elysian Park is the second largest of Los Angeles' parks and contains hiking trails and a lake as well as children's playgrounds. But the main reason that most people visit Elysian Park is to see the Dodgers play. The stadium, which was built in 1963, is a Los Angeles landmark, and as an outing it is a unique experience for your kids.

There is something quite amazing about being in a crowd of fifty thousand people doing the wave, singing "Take Me Out to the Ballgame," cheering, and booing. Which brings me to my next point: why are the fans *so* rude? My five-year-old turned to me at one point during the game and said, "Is this the team we have to hate?"

**RATING**

**ADDRESS/PHONE/WEB SITE**
1000 Elysian Park Avenue
Los Angeles 90012
323-224-1HIT

**COST**
Varies; generally $6 and up per ticket

**PARKING**
$10

**HOURS**
Varies with game

**STROLLER ACCESS**
Adequate for a single stroller

**MORE THAN ONE ADULT NEEDED?**
Yes

**RECOMMENDATION**
This is an experience—who cares who wins?

Make sure whatever tickets you purchase are on the aisle since you'll be jumping up twenty times during the game to get your kid another hot dog, take another trip to the bathroom, or just relieve the boredom. The game can be viewed on TVs set up on the balconies, and it's piped into the bathroom via a sound system. So it's easy enough to keep up with the play, even if you are chasing your toddler around and around the concrete balcony. You won't be alone; amongst the beer swillers and smokers who can't smoke in the stadium itself there are always toddlers being pushed in strollers or on the loose. Games do run late, but if you don't care about the final score, or are pretty sure you know the outcome, leave early! Getting out of the parking lot is challenging, and if the gods are with you, your kids will fall asleep in the car by the time you leave.

## Echo Park

This little inner-city park is right off the freeway. It features a lake with paddle boats and ducks. There is a playground, picnic area, and a year-round swimming pool. But what separates this park from most in the city and happily makes it unique are the lotus flowers growing on one end of the lake. Every year in July, the Lotus Festival is held, complete with Chinese dragon boats, Polynesian dancing, martial arts exhibits, and huge crowds. There is also a Cuban festival, held in late May. I've never been able to find parking for either event, so I would suggest taking the Metro.

RATING

ADDRESS/PHONE/WEB SITE
1632 Bellevue Avenue
Los Angeles 90026
213-250-3578

COST
Free unless swimming or renting a boat

PARKING
Free

HOURS
Open daily, 7:00 a.m.–10:00 p.m.

STROLLER ACCESS
Adequate for a double-wide stroller

MORE THAN ONE ADULT NEEDED?
No

THE LOWDOWN
Take the Metro if you're headed to any major event like one of the festivals they hold here.

## Little Tokyo/Japanese American National Museum

Little Tokyo is more subtle than Chinatown; it's a smaller, less commercial venue. Little Tokyo's biggest structure is the Japanese American National Museum.

This beautiful building is dedicated to the preservation of the Japanese American experience and, in particular, to the internment in camps of so many Japanese Americans during World War II. In this respect, this is a vitally important museum that everyone should make an effort to see.

However, much like the Museum of Tolerance and the Holocaust Museum, this isn't really a place to bring small children. There is a lesson to be learned here, but it is not a hands-on or visually stimulating one, so let the kids grow a little and take them when they are old enough to understand and read the placards, or go without them.

**RATING**

**ADDRESS/PHONE/WEB SITE**

369 East First Street
Los Angeles 90012
213-625-0141
www.janm.org

**COST**

Adults, $8; seniors, $5; students (with ID) and children ages 6–17, $4; free every Thursday from 5:00 p.m.–8:00 p.m. and every third Thursday of the month

**PARKING**

$4.25 at the corner of First and Central

**HOURS**

Tue–Sun, 10:00 a.m.–5:00 p.m.; Thu, 10:00 a.m.–8:00 p.m.; closed Mondays, New Year's Day, Thanksgiving, and Christmas

**STROLLER ACCESS**

Adequate for up to a double-wide stroller

**MORE THAN ONE ADULT NEEDED?**

No

**THE LOWDOWN**

See if you can get to one of their family days; the New Year's celebration (in January) is probably the biggest and it's free.

All this being said, the museum does host temporary exhibits downstairs. The last one I went to featured wooden furniture. This exhibit was set up to be as child friendly as possible, with a guide directed at parents with children and, at the end, an area where you could touch different kinds of wood and sit on the furniture. So, if there is a temporary exhibit at the museum, it may be suitable for kids. Check the Web site for a schedule. Also, they host occasional family days where the kids can make arts and crafts, hear stories, and experience a different culture.

While you're in Little Tokyo you can check out the cute knick-knacks, and it's a great place for lunch. My personal favorite is the red bean ice cream.

# Los Angeles Central Library

The Los Angeles Central Library is worth a visit just because it is a beautiful structure, a classic old building added onto with thought and care. Even if all you do is climb into the old, clean, shiny brass elevators and go up to the mural-painted rotunda and into the children's area, you will all have a great time. The children's wing, unlike most kids' areas in libraries, is isolated from the rest of the library, so that when your kids forget to use their "quiet voice" for the millionth time, it's not so bad.

The library has a great collection of foreign language children's books (not just the usual Spanish and English ones found in most libraries). In addition, the Central Library hosts children's puppet shows as well as various special exhibits.

Take your kids to the library, and be prepared to stay a while reading oversized picture books and putting books that your toddler has very carefully strewn about back on the shelves.

**RATING**

**ADDRESS/PHONE/WEB SITE**
630 West Fifth Street
Los Angeles 90071
213-228-7000

**COST**
Free

**PARKING**
The library validates for parking at 524 South Flower Street and 550 South Hope Street and ranges from $1 up, depending upon time of day and lot used. (It is still easier to take the Metro downtown than drive in and park, so call 1-800-COMMUTE.)

**HOURS**
Mon–Thu, 10:00 a.m.–8:00 p.m.; Fri–Sat, 10:00 a.m.–6:00 p.m.; Sun, 1:00 p.m.–5:00 p.m.

**STROLLER ACCESS**
Totally accessible for up to a double-wide stroller

**MORE THAN ONE ADULT NEEDED?**
No

**THE LOWDOWN**
Try to see one of the shows. Take your kids to your local library first, so they can learn library manners.

# Los Angeles Music Center

Los Angeles is trying very hard to be cultural, and to that extent the Walt Disney Concert Hall has joined the group of theaters that make up the Los Angeles Music Center: the Dorothy Chandler Pavilion, the Mark Taper Forum, and the Ahmanson Theatre. This latest addition is the most unique building you will ever enter. Its construction raised more than a few comments of the "love it or hate it" variety, but now that it's finished there is a real effort to involve Southern Californians in it.

Throughout the fall, winter, and spring the Walt Disney Concert Hall hosts the World City series of free concerts of international music. Having attended their concerts last year, let me give you a few hints: (1) arrive early; (2) don't take any kid that's scared of the dark or of heights into the concert hall; and (3) there is an arts and crafts area set up across the street where they have more music playing, and you won't have to enter the dark concert hall.

**RATING**

**ADDRESS/PHONE/WEB SITE**

Grand Ave between Temple and Second Street
213-972-7211
www.musiccenter.org

**COST**

Free for World music events, cost for shows vary; Pillow Theater is currently $10 each or $28 for four shows

**PARKING**

$8 for event parking, or up to $17/day. (Downtown is best reached by Metro, call 1-800-COMMUTE to find your best route.)

**HOURS**

Vary upon event

**STROLLER ACCESS**

Adequate until you cross the street to the Dorothy Chandler Pavilion; then locating the elevator is harder than finding someone to help you carry the stroller up the stairs.

**MORE THAN ONE ADULT NEEDED?**

No

**THE LOWDOWN**

Go to the free events; they are incredible and FREE! If your kids enjoy them and prove they can sit still long enough for a real show, Pillow Theater is worth the money. Check the Web site for upcoming events.

We, of course, arrived late the first time, rushed upstairs through this glorious building only to find our seats somewhere near the top. But the minute my four-year-old looked down into the pit with musicians playing before us, she wanted nothing to do with it. Had we arrived early and reached our seats while the lights were still on or found a seat lower in the hall, she probably would have been fine. However, the outside events were more than worthwhile, so make the effort and show your kids some culture—it's free.

If you enjoy the free events, you might consider buying tickets to the Pillow Theatre. Aimed at three- to six-year-olds, the shows feature music, theater and dance, and storytelling. There is an arts and crafts project for the kids to do after the show.

# MOCA (Museum of Contempory Art)/Geffen Contemporary/ Pacific Design Center

One museum at three locations.

No, three locations isn't a great idea; it just appears to be a way to expand without actually expanding. Here's how it works: if you buy a ticket to one of the locations and are willing to drive to the other locations and pay for parking *yet again,* the entry to the other locations will be free on the same day. I'm not going to drag my kids in and out of three art galleries on the same day, but hey, maybe you'd like to try it. (Frankly, even I'm not all that crazy about traipsing through three galleries in one day, but maybe I'm not the norm.)

Since these are contemporary art galleries, the guards don't follow you around the way they do at art galleries that feature priceless antiquities, and the art itself is changing, often fun and imaginative. My daughter's favorite when we went was the chocolate room (a room covered in chocolate covered paper—it smelled great). Just remember these are art galleries, lots of "look don't touch," so be prepared to move quickly through the exhibits.

**RATING**

**ADDRESS/PHONE/WEB SITE**

California Plaza: 250 South Grand Avenue, Los Angeles 90012
The Geffen Contemporary: 152 North Central Avenue, Los Angeles 90013
Pacific Design Center: 8687 Melrose Avenue, West Hollywood 90069
General: 213-626-6222
Visitor Services: 213-621-1741

**COST**

General admission, $8 (Valid for all locations on the date of purchase); students and seniors (65+), $5; children under 12, free; free on Thursdays

**PARKING**

Available in nearby lots for approximately $5

**HOURS**

Mon, 11:00 a.m.–5:00 p.m.; Tue–Wed, closed; Thu, 11:00 a.m.–8:00 p.m. (free); Fri, 11:00 a.m.–5:00 p.m.; Sat–Sun, 11:00 a.m.–6:00 p.m.; Closed New Year's Day, Independence Day, Thanksgiving, and Christmas

**STROLLER ACCESS**

Adequate for up to a double-wide stroller

**MORE THAN ONE ADULT NEEDED?**

No

**THE LOWDOWN**

Go on the free day. At the California Plaza location, take a stroller you can fold up, so that you don't have to take the wheelchair lift.

## MOCA CALIFORNIA PLAZA

This gallery is located underground, and to get in you'll have to take the stroller up a wheelchair lift to the offices and then descend via the "employees only" elevator. Once inside there are steps that can be avoided if you just reverse and go all the way around. Downstairs is the family discovery room, which looks like a '60s modern living room, and which is not set up for young kids at all. The books are aimed at adults and older children. Overall, the whole place looks like it desperately needs to be refurbished. It is stroller and wheelchair accessible—but only just.

## MOCA THE GEFFEN CONTEMPORARY

About a mile away in Little Tokyo is the Geffen Contemporary. It was originally dubbed the Temporary Contemporary, and it feels temporary, more like a dark warehouse than an art gallery. It does, however, have great stroller access.

## MOCA PACIFIC DESIGN CENTER

You'll find this museum in West Hollywood. It features architecture and design exhibits.

# Natural History Museum

This is one of the best places in L.A. County to take your kids on a wet day. What kid isn't going to love dinosaur bones and stuffed lions and elephants? No, seriously. My daughter has books about moose and beaver, but this was the first time she really saw them. Personally, I think it's better than the zoo; at least we could see the bear because it wasn't hiding. Sure, it wasn't alive, but it was no more sedentary than the one at the zoo. Seriously though, this is a great museum in a beautiful old building.

Find the Discovery Center. Your kids could spend the whole day in this room alone. Leave your stroller in the stroller park, and let your kids roam. From marine aquariums to shells, skins, and bones they can touch, this is a truly kid-friendly learning environment. At the rear of the room there is a stage where a young tortoise wanders, and kids (over age two) can touch him. Then there is the Dig Pit, where they can "find" fossils. Even my one-year-old was intrigued by this and used a brush to fling the artificial sand off the plastic fossils. There are snakes,

**RATING**

**ADDRESS/PHONE/WEB SITE**
900 Exposition Boulevard
Los Angeles 90007 (between Vermont and Figueroa)
213-763-DINO
www.nhm.org

**COST**
Adults, $9.00; seniors (62+), $6.50; children 13–17 and students, $6.50; children 5–12, $2.00; under 5, free; first Tuesday of every month is free

**PARKING**
$6

**HOURS**
Mon–Fri, 9:30 a.m.–5:00 p.m.; Sat–Sun, and holidays, 10 a.m.–5:00 p.m.

**STROLLER ACCESS**
Adequate, but this is an old building, so you may find if you don't want to take stairs that the restroom or the elevator is sometimes a hike.

**MORE THAN ONE ADULT NEEDED?**
No

**THE LOWDOWN**
Buy a membership; you are going to want to go back—and so are your kids. The entry fee is high, but a membership for a family for a year is only $60 and will also give you access to the La Brea Tar Pits/George Page Museum and the William S. Hart Museum and Ranch. The museum closes at five, and I usually can't get my kids to leave until then. This is, of course, the worst time to drive through downtown L.A., so I would suggest using the nearby Metro to get there. Check www.MTA.net for exact times, or call 1-800-COMMUTE.

tortoises, and a stuffed alligator kids can touch. You may find that your kids don't want to see the real animals, because they are far too busy playing with the games and puzzles laid out for them on the tables or doing an arts and crafts project.

When they have touched, banged, and tasted everything, the insect zoo is upstairs (not stroller friendly, but we can't have every-thing—leave it parked and carry the kids). There they can see lots of creepy spiders and roaches. As soon as you are done with that, sneak your kids out of the Discovery Center while you can. There is so much more to see that you and the kids will be tired before you explore everything.

Open every year from May to September is the Butterfly Pavilion. This and the gemstones are my daughters' favorites. And although I, for one, would love to go explore the Ancient Latin Culture hall, appar-ently old ceramics aren't as fun as butterflies and gold and diamonds.

A lot of the museum is very dark and atmospheric (in order to show off the exhibits), so let the kids run outside on the grass before you get back in your car. And remember: this is downtown L.A.; try not to get caught in traffic on the way home.

# Olvera Street/Union Station

OK, they are not the same place. But you shouldn't see one without the other. Union Station is a beautiful old railroad station, well-maintained and featured in many films from your youth, although none of this is going to excite your toddlers very much. It is, however, across the street from Olvera Street. If you are anywhere near a Metro line, I recommend taking a train into Union Station and walking across to Olvera Street. It makes a nice day trip.

On the weekends you will find Olvera Street a very busy Mexican marketplace, but you should be able to negotiate a single stroller through the narrow alleyways between vendors—probably.

Olvera Street is the birthplace of Los Angeles and has twenty-seven historic buildings. These, of course, are *L.A.* historic, not *European* historic, so they are only a few hundred years old. Make sure you find the Avila Adobe; it is the oldest structure still standing in

**RATING**
🪑🪑🪑🪑

**ADDRESS/PHONE/WEB SITE**
Union Station: 800 N. Alameda Street, Los Angeles 90012
El Pueblo de Los Angeles/Olvera Street: 845 N. Alameda Street, Los Angeles
213-628-3562
www.cityofla.org/elp

**COST**
Free

**PARKING**
Approximately $4 to $10, the cheapest is at 711 N. Alameda St

**HOURS**
The street is open 10:00 a.m.–7:00 p.m.; the Avila Adobe closes at 3:00 p.m.

**STROLLER ACCESS**
It's often very crowded, so take a single umbrella stroller; be prepared to carry your kids in some of the historic sites

**MORE THAN ONE ADULT NEEDED?**
No

**THE LOWDOWN**
You may want to try this on a weekday when it is not as packed. On the weekend, getting into the restaurants for lunch requires a long wait, and, though the food from the taquerias is passable, it's far from the best Mexican food L.A. has to offer.

L.A., built in 1819. It closes at 3:00, so get there while it's open. Donations are requested to go inside this building, which is furnished as it would have been in the day. There is no stroller access in the building, and you'll end up carrying the kids so they don't try to climb on the antiques. It's great for them to see how life has changed. My four-year-

21

old made me go back through the house a second time, but even after two visits I am not sure she believed me when I told her that kids back then only had one doll.

The market and vendor aspect can distract from the historic, but there are free docent-led tours Wednesday through Saturday each hour from 10:00 a.m. until 12:00 p.m. If your kids are like mine, a better bet may be the self-guided tour. A brochure describing the historic buildings is available at the information desk in the plaza or at the El Pueblo Visitor Center located in the Sepulveda House, midway down Olvera Street on the west side.

The Visitor Center also has an eighteen-minute film entitled "Pueblo of Promise" about the history and development of the City of Los Angeles. I haven't seen it all the way through, because eighteen minutes is a long show when it's not animated, but if you feel lucky, try to catch it.

On the weekends there are often special events in the square, the biggest being Cinco de Mayo. Even without these there is more than you will be able to do in one day; admission is free so you can come back as often as you like. All it will cost you is a toy for the kids, food, and a tip for the wandering mariachi band.

## Wells Fargo History Museum

If you are downtown, this place is worth finding. Tucked in behind a Wells Fargo bank in a courtyard off the street is this small, free museum. The museum is based around the history of the Wells Fargo Company, which in many ways is a history of the West. From the earliest gold miners (gold pans and nuggets on display) to the stagecoaches that brought people west and the banks that became part of the civilization of the new territories, this little museum has something for even the youngest child.

An 1880s stagecoach sits at the entrance, and although the small sign telling you not to touch is completely lost on the young (who are invariably irritated at being told no), in the rear of the museum is a full-size replica that more than makes up for it. You are not only invited to climb inside the replica, but once inside you can bounce it around, simulating an actual bumpy stagecoach ride across country. This is one of those untimed, self-propelled rides, and if you are the only people there—as we were—then you can bump and sway until you have pretended to cross the entire country.

When everyone is good and seasick, on the other side of the museum is a replica of an early bank, complete with a telegraph machine and code book so that your little ones can play. A complete tour of the museum won't take long, but it will be fun.

**RATING**

**ADDRESS/PHONE/WEB SITE**
333 South Grand Avenue
Los Angeles 90071
213-253-7166

**COST**
Free

**PARKING**
Varies, approximately $6

**HOURS**
Mon–Fri, 9:00 a.m.–5:00 p.m.

**STROLLER ACCESS**
Adequate for a double-wide stroller

**MORE THAN ONE ADULT NEEDED?**
No

**THE LOWDOWN**
Make sure you check this one out if you are downtown, or combine it with another downtown location for a day trip.

# Hollywood/Griffith Park/
# Mount Washington

# Barnsdall Art Park/Hollyhock House

In Hollywood, hidden behind Kaiser Hospital, is Barnsdall Art Park. In addition to the Los Angeles Municipal Art Gallery, a small art gallery with changing exhibits and a theater, the park also boasts Hollyhock House, Frank Lloyd Wright's first project in Los Angeles.

The art gallery features modern artists and is not geared toward children. In fact, the last time we went there was a notice that one of the two exhibits was unsuitable for children. What this means exactly, I don't know, because the exhibit that *was* supposed to be suitable contained two pieces that looked very much like human genitalia (my oldest daughter noticed them, and I convinced her they were an ear and a strange-looking tree) and a display of glass balls lying in a field of sand (my youngest wanted to play with them so much it hurt).

Hollyhock House was a surprise to me. I thought, because of the name, that it would be a cute, pretty structure; instead it is more like an Aztec temple. The house is only open for scheduled exterior tours and is currently undergoing restoration. Unless you have the kind of children who enjoy hour-long speeches about architectural history, this probably isn't the place for them.

RATING

ADDRESS/PHONE/WEB SITE
4800 Hollywood Blvd
Los Angeles 90027
323-644-6275

COST
Varies

PARKING
Free

HOURS
Wed–Sun, 12:00–5:00 p.m.

STROLLER ACCESS
Adequate for a double-wide stroller

MORE THAN ONE ADULT NEEDED?
No

THE LOWDOWN
They have a junior art program, but it is aimed at older children. This place just isn't designed for preschoolers.

# El Capitan Theatre

The El Capitan was a beautiful movie palace when it was first built in 1926, and after all the money Disney has poured into it, the glory and grandeur has been reborn. Of course, because it is Disney, the place is more than just a pretty movie theater. In addition to a movie, when you buy a ticket for the latest Disney flick at El Capitan, you get to see a live organist and a stage show.

The last time my family went, we loved the live show and the organist. My oldest, who hated the movie, wanted to know why we didn't leave after the live show. (The real answer: although I hated the movie too, I had a sleeping baby in my arms and it was just easier to stay).

**RATING**

**ADDRESS/PHONE/WEB SITE**
6838 Hollywood Blvd
Hollywood 90028
1-800-DISNEY6

**COST**
General admission: $15 or $24

**PARKING**
$2 at Hollywood and Highland

**HOURS**
Check the movie listings (online or in the newspaper)

**STROLLER ACCESS**
Adequate for up to a double-wide stroller

**MORE THAN ONE ADULT NEEDED?**
No

**THE LOWDOWN**
Go midweek and pay $15 the next time a good Disney movie comes out.

The shows at the El Capitan are great, so if the movie stinks and you want to leave, you will still get your money's worth. There are, however, some tricks to attending a film at the El Capitan. All seats (including kids tickets) when there is a live show are either $15 or $24. For $24 you get to sit in preferred seating, but if you go there on a weekday to an uncrowded film, then you can sit in these preferred seats for a mere $15.

It's an expensive movie, but the added bonus of the live show makes it worthwhile.

# Grauman's Chinese Theatre/Hollywood Boulevard

Hollywood Boulevard is a mecca for tourists, and it can be a fun day even for locals. Hollywood and Highland is the new mall, featuring a great view of the Hollywood sign and an interesting "road to Hollywood" trail; my kids love to climb on the concrete casting couch at the end. Driving and parking in Hollywood can be difficult, and if you have access to the Metro I would recommend taking the Red Line train and getting off at the subway station underneath the mall.

Next door to the mall is Grauman's Chinese Theatre, where stars have been dipping their hands and feet in cement since 1927. The forecourt of the theatre is free of charge, and during the weekend it can be a complete zoo, with tourists tripping over each other trying to see how their feet compare to John Wayne's. Little kids like this game of stepping into old footprints, but the significance of Marilyn Monroe or Arnold Schwarzenegger is pretty much lost on kids who will grow up thinking that Schwarzenegger was always a politician. So plan on continuing down the Boulevard pretty swiftly. The theatre does give tours, but I've never seen a tour guide who can keep preschoolers interested in architecture and history. If you think your child will enjoy it, by all means try.

In recent years Hollywood Boulevard has become cleaner, safer, and more trafficked. Most people attribute at least part of this to the Disney effect. Disney bought the **El Capitan Theatre** across the street

**RATING**

**ADDRESS/PHONE/WEB SITE**
Hollywood Blvd around Highland
Hollywood

**COST**
Free

**PARKING**
As little as $2 at Hollywood and Highland

**HOURS**
Varies by venue

**STROLLER ACCESS**
Adequate for up to a double-wide stroller

**MORE THAN ONE ADULT NEEDED?**
No

**THE LOWDOWN**
The Metro is a great way to get to this area (call 1-800-COMMUTE or check www.mta.net).

and restored it to its earlier glory. Further down the boulevard you will also find the restored Egyptian Theatre.

Across from Grauman's is another, usually less crowded, Hollywood landmark, the Roosevelt Hotel. Step into the lobby and it feels like you are back in the glory days of Hollywood. On the mezzanine there is a photo display of Hollywood's history. Take a break from the crowds, come in with the kids, and enjoy a soda in 1930s glory.

As you travel down the street you'll see many street performers and actors in costume advertising various venues. Many of these actors are just plain scary for young kids. Last time we went, both the creepy mask-wearing guy from *Scream* and the Green Goblin from *Spiderman* scared my daughter, so be aware of this. There will definitely be acts that they'll love too, though. There is usually a mime in front of the **Hollywood Wax Museum,** and my kids love to watch him as he freezes and then reanimates. Other places in Hollywood include the **Ripley's Believe It or Not! Museum**, the **Hollywood Entertainment Museum, Los Angeles Fire Department Museum**, the **Hollywood History Museum,** and the **Guinness World of Records Museum.**

# Griffith Observatory and Satellite Facility

The Griffith Observatory, which was formerly one of my favorite places to take both my kids and guests from out of town, is closed for renovations until 2006. I wish I didn't have to wait that long. The exhibits were fun and educational, from the huge pendulum in the foyer which showed how the earth is turning, to the smaller exhibits that demonstrated the seasons or the gravity well. Everyone I have ever taken there, even babies, loved the observatory.

The observatory has always been free, except for the planetarium show. My daughter is scared of the dark, so it has been some time since I have actually seen the planetarium show, although I did pay for it once (oh boy, did I pay). The lights went out, and I had to stumble through the dark carrying a crying baby.

**RATING**

**ADDRESS/PHONE/WEB SITE**
Griffith Park
Los Angeles 90027
323-664-1181

**COST**
Free

**PARKING**
Free

**HOURS**
Satellite office: Tue–Fri, 1:00 p.m.–10:00 p.m.; Sat–Sun, 10:00 a.m.–10:00 p.m.; Planetarium: Fri, 7:00–9:00 p.m.; Sat, 1:00–9:00 p.m.; Sun, 1:00–5:00 p.m.

**STROLLER ACCESS**
Adequate for a double-wide stroller

**MORE THAN ONE ADULT NEEDED?**
No

**THE LOWDOWN**
I'll meet you in line on the day it reopens.

There are telescopes to look through at the waning stars in the L.A. sky, but without ever looking in a telescope, the greatest spectacle of lights could always be seen from the rear of the building as you looked down on the city at night. The new additions and renovations sound great: a new presentation theater, two new exhibit areas, improvements to the planetarium, a new on-site café, better stroller and handicapped access through the building, and more restrooms. (Quite frankly, the restrooms were always the only thing that ever marred a trip to the observatory.) Perhaps the new and improved restrooms will even have a diaper changing table; given that they are spending over $80 million fixing the old place up, I hope they put an extra few hundred in for at least two of these.

Until the observatory reopens, they are running a satellite facility out of a relocatable trailer near the zoo. The satellite facility has a few meteorites and pictures of the construction. It even has a large model of the moon and Mars, but it is just not much of a thrill. Will the real observatory please open again? Please! On Friday night, and on the weekend, they run a small planetarium; this could be fun for little ones. It's sort of a low commitment, low scare version of a real planetarium. The show runs about thirty minutes and has no real agenda, so the lecturer will answer questions and tell you what you want to know. The entire satellite facility is free, so try it out on a weekend, and see if your kids will watch the planetarium light show—if they won't, there are plenty of other things to do in Griffith Park.

# Griffith Park

Griffith Park is not only the largest city park in America, it is also home to many attractions.

As a parent, the ones that will interest you most are the **Museum of the American West,** the **Griffith Observatory,** the **Los Angeles Zoo, Travel Town, L.A. Live Steamers, Griffith Park Merry-Go-Round,** and the **Pony Ride and Southern Railroad.**

But first, the park itself. It's huge, it's hilly, and much of it is untouched land that you can hike through, as long as your kids are good hikers or good at sitting in a backpack carrier. This part isn't necessarily stroller territory, but most of the park is. In fact, some to the best and most affordable places to take young kids in L.A. are located in Griffith Park.

## SHANE'S INSPIRATION

This is a huge playground complex within the park. Follow the signs to the merry-go-round and you

**RATING**
Park:
Merry-Go-Round:

**ADDRESS/PHONE/WEB SITE**
4730 Crystal Springs Drive
Los Angeles 90027
323-913-4688

**COST**
Park, free; Merry-Go-Round, $1.50 per person

**PARKING**
Free

**HOURS**
Park, 6:00 a.m.–10:00 p.m. every day; Merry-Go-Round, 11:00–5:00 p.m. weekends and vacations, and weekdays during the summer

**STROLLER ACCESS**
Adequate for up to a double-wide stroller

**MORE THAN ONE ADULT NEEDED?**
No

**THE LOWDOWN**
At Christmas time my kids love to drive through the DWP Festival of Lights. It starts at the Los Feliz entrance, and it's free. It can be slow going but seems to be less crowded just before Christmas than earlier in December.

will find it. There is plenty of parking. This play area was designed to be suitable for a handicapped child, so this makes the equipment some of the safest and most toddler friendly I have seen. The downside is that the play area is huge and unfenced. Every time I go there I find myself chasing different children in different directions, screaming things like, "Where is your sister?" "Don't run off on me!" "Stay together." You get the idea. On the weekends the play area is very crowded, and it's easy to misplace a child or two, so you will have to play with your kids or keep them on a very short leash. The good news is there are restroom facilities—nowhere to change babies, of course, but I get happy if a park even has a potty.

## MERRY-GO-ROUND

The Griffith Park Merry-Go-Round is located near the play area. It was built in 1926 and is a beautiful work of art. However, unlike other carousels, every horse on this carousel moves, and having ridden it myself, let me say that they move up and down and round and round very, very fast! I also found the calliope music to be extremely loud. So keep your kids off this one if motion or loud noise upsets them.

## Guinness World of Records Museum

The Guinness World of Records Museum is of little interest to young kids, simply because it is set up almost like the book it is based on. You walk, you look at a picture or a display, and unless you can read what is written next to it, it means nothing. And even if you *can* read what's next to it, it isn't a thrill. Maybe it's just me, but learning that Mickey Mouse got the most fan mail does not fascinate me.

The most interesting display was a model of the world's tallest man and the world's smallest woman, which were together. Which inevitably led to questions like "Why was he so tall?" "Did he hit his head on the ceiling?" "If I don't eat enough will I stop growing now and shrink to her size?" Little kids aren't really ready for this place; if they understand it at all, they find it somewhat disturbing.

We were on our way to the second floor in a musty old elevator that would not work when my daughter told me she was already scared and wanted to leave *now*. I was so bored I was happy to oblige.

**RATING**

**ADDRESS/PHONE/WEB SITE**
6764 Hollywood Boulevard
Hollywood 90028
323-463-6433

**COST**
Adults, $10.95; seniors (64+), $8.50; children 6–12, $6.95; combined with Hollywood Wax Museum: Adults, $15.95; seniors, $13.95; children, $8.95

**PARKING**
$2 at Hollywood and Highland

**HOURS**
Sun–Thu, 10:00 a.m.–midnight; Fri–Sat, 10:00 a.m.–1:00 a.m.

**STROLLER ACCESS**
Adequate for up to a double-wide stroller

**MORE THAN ONE ADULT NEEDED?**
No

**THE LOWDOWN**
Why would you go here with small kids?

## Heritage Square

On the side of the 110 freeway, going north towards Pasadena, there is an odd collection of buildings. This is Heritage Square. Gathered from all over the city, these buildings (which date from 1850–1950) were saved from demolition to demonstrate architecture and changing styles in this parklike setting.

The buildings range from fully restored with period furnishings to still needs the first coat of paint. Tours are given on the hour, and unless you go on the tour you can only see the exterior of the buildings. It has been my experience that young kids are not as appreciative of an hourlong talk about architectural features as one might wish. Also, most of the buildings are not stroller accessible, even if your little one has crashed out and you think you'll be left in peace long enough to finish the tour. So if you want to go, take a picnic lunch and someone who is willing to entertain the kids outside while you take the tour.

If you decide not to take the tour, the admission price is usually waived and they ask for a donation instead. You will find it a great place for a picnic, and the restrooms have old-fashioned toilets with long flushing chains that will fascinate most kids.

**RATING**

**ADDRESS/PHONE/WEB SITE**
3800 Homer Street
Pasadena 91101
626-449-0193

**COST**
Adults, $10; seniors, $8; children 6–12, $5; includes tour

**PARKING**
Free

**HOURS**
Open Fri–Sun and most holiday Mondays; summer hours: 12:00 to 5:00 p.m.; winter hours: 11:30 a.m.–4:30 p.m.; closed New Year's Day, Thanksgiving, and Christmas

**STROLLER ACCESS**
Inadequate; these are historic buildings with stairs

**MORE THAN ONE ADULT NEEDED?**
No

**THE LOWDOWN**
If you want to see the buildings, leave the kids with a sitter.

# Hollywood Bowl

The Hollywood Bowl is an experience, but unless you plan well it won't necessarily be a pleasant one. The Bowl offers several shows throughout the summer season that are aimed at children. There is also a summer program for children called **Summer Sounds,** which I will cover separately.

Tickets for shows at the Bowl are affordable. In fact, they can be less expensive than a movie. My advice is to get the cheapest seats you can and buy some binoculars. You'll doubtless find that many of the patrons in the nosebleed seats have also brought their kids, and if yours need to run up and down the stairs, they'll have company and room to roam up there in the stratosphere.

Parking at the Bowl means sitting in a huge traffic jam and then being stack-parked, nose to tail, so that after the show you have to wait until everyone ahead of you clears out. A show that starts at 8:30 will leave you in your car, in the parking lot, still waiting to exit at midnight. Maybe you'll be lucky and your kids will be asleep, but more than likely this will be the one night they are having a screaming fit while you sit in the lot. One way to avoid this is to use the Park and Ride, but beware: they stack-park cars in those lots too. So, if possible, park your car outside the Park and Ride lot.

RATING

ADDRESS/PHONE/WEB SITE
2301 North Highland Boulevard
Hollywood 90078
323-850-2000
www.hollywoodbowl.com

COST
Tickets range from $6 on up, depending upon the event

PARKING
$11–$13, unless you take the Park and Ride—then it is free, but the bus fare is $5 per person

STROLLER ACCESS
Adequate for a single umbrella stroller you can fold up and put at your feet

HOURS
Depends upon event

MORE THAN ONE ADULT NEEDED?
Yes

THE LOWDOWN
Try out the rehearsal sessions with your kids before you invest in a long, long night. Call the bowl for rehearsal times and details.

However, should you decide to use Park and Ride, you cannot—I repeat, *cannot*—leave the show before it is over, because there are no buses. Your very mature four-year-old may be sick of the show after an hour, and you will still have two hours left, plus a wait, plus a bus ride. Your very best bet with kids is to take your cell phone and have someone who owes you a big favor fight the traffic, drop you off at the Bowl, and pick you up. If you have ever seen the Hollywood Bowl traffic, you will realize that this patron saint of dropoffs has to really owe you, because it is comparable to taking someone to LAX. So if you haven't taken your brother/father/friend to the airport lately, start building up some brownie points now. A slightly less painful option might be to have them drop you at the Park and Ride and pick you up at the Bowl; for this favor you probably only need to look after their cat when they go out of town.

Also, no matter how warm it was before you went out, by the time the show is half over your kids will be freezing. Dress the kids warmly, bring blankets, and pray that at some point they just fall asleep. The seats are bleachers so the extra clothes and blankets you bring can also serve as cushions. Also, the Bowl has a tradition of being a picnic spot before the show. Take advantage of this; you do not want to spend twenty dollars on a chocolate bar, bag of chips, and a soda. Bring lots of food and drink.

Don't try this without preparation. It also helps to have kids who will go to sleep (not cry) when their bedtimes are long past. So, have I scared you yet? Well, wait—here's a secret: If you go to the Bowl in the morning before a show, you can watch a rehearsal. You will get to see the show for free, with no parking nightmare, no freezing night air, and no six-dollar sodas! Of course, you also won't get to see a fireworks spectacular (although for some kids this is a plus!), or experience the thrill of being part of an audience, but you have kids—this may be as good as it gets.

# Hollywood Entertainment Museum

Once you get down the elevator, you will find this modern museum buried under the Galaxy movie theaters. As you enter, there are models of some of the movies' all-time scariest monsters, and believe me, even inanimate and behind glass the creature from *Aliens* still scares the willies out of me. This pretty much tells you right off the bat that this museum was never intended for children.

The rest of the exhibits are interesting enough, but the real museum is in the backlot, a tour that comes free with paid admission. In addition to a working video editing and Foley sound room, where you can actually learn more about the movie-making process, the tour will take you through their impressive and entertaining collection of props.

The props are laid out warehouse-style, and they ask you not to touch—just try making a two-year-old understand that. In the very first room you enter there are fake dismembered body parts, super gross for the susceptible. Then you go through their wardrobe section, but by the time people figured out that the suit on the end was worn by Whoopi Goldberg in *Ghost,* my kids were done with the tour. I never got to see the pièces de résistance of the

**RATING**

**ADDRESS/PHONE/WEB SITE**
7021 Hollywood Boulevard
Hollywood 90028
323-465-7900

**COST**
Adults, $8.75; seniors, $5.50; students, $4.50; children age 5–12, $4

**PARKING**
$2 at Hollywood and Vine if you get validation

**HOURS**
11:00 a.m.–6:00 p.m.; open daily in the summer; closed Wed in the winter and on New Year's Day, Thanksgiving, and Christmas

**STROLLER ACCESS**
The tour through the backlot is not suitable for strollers.

**MORE THAN ONE ADULT NEEDED?**
No

**THE LOWDOWN**
This is an expensive museum best done with adults only. If your kids can pay attention for a one-hour guided tour and are brave in the face of special effects, then give it a go.

museum, the entire *Cheers* bar set and the bridge from the Starship *Enterprise*. My kids didn't care, and they had no idea why I did either.

This is a great museum; just leave your kids with a sitter so that you can really enjoy it.

# Hollywood Wax Museum

The Hollywood Wax Museum is full of wax statues of celebrities. This won't necessarily impress your kids; after all, who are these people to them? The statues my daughters liked best were the ones that can be seen for free in the lobby: Dorothy, the Tin Man, the Scarecrow, the Cowardly Lion, and Toto. These wax sculptures will provide an answer to that all-important question: do almost-lifelike figures with dead eyes scare your kids?

As long as your child isn't horrified by the stillness of the figures, the museum is somewhat considerate—at least their "Chamber of Horrors" is located on its own loop, so that you can avoid it altogether.

There is a special if you purchase this museum and **Guinness World of Records** together. Both of these museums are little more than run-down sideshows that are attempting to fleece the tourists, but if you feel the need to see Michael Jackson in all his '80s glory (when he was still brown and had a nose), this is the place.

**RATING**

**ADDRESS/PHONE/WEB SITE**
6767 Hollywood Boulevard
Hollywood 90028
323-462-5991

**COST**
Adults, $10.95; seniors (64+), $8.50; children 6–12, $6.95. Children (6-12) $6.95; combined with Guinness World of Records: Adults, $15.95; seniors, $13.95; children, $8.95

**PARKING**
$2 at Hollywood and Highland

**HOURS**
Sun–Thu, 10:00 a.m.–midnight; Fri–Sat, 10:00 a.m.–1:00 a.m.

**STROLLER ACCESS**
Adequate for up to a double-wide stroller

**MORE THAN ONE ADULT NEEDED?**
No

**THE LOWDOWN**
Save the money and go to the park instead.

# Los Angeles Fire Department Museum

My oldest rated this place an 11 out of 10, and compared to the other attractions in the Hollywood area the praise is not undeserved. This new museum displays a variety of firefighting equipment in a historic fire station. Downstairs there are fire engines, ambulances, and horse-drawn ladder trucks. For my youngest, the biggest thrill was pushing a button and turning on the flashing lights, although the free fire hats the kids were given ran a pretty close second.

In addition to the real engines there are model engines. The downstairs is not particularly child-safe, but they are trying, and they are friendly and welcoming—when your two-year-old doesn't read the "Do Not Touch" sign, slips under the rope, and starts to climb up to drive the fire engine, they will help you get her down, not look at you as if you're the worst parent on earth.

The best part of the whole museum is upstairs. There is a large open room, where your kid can try on fire boots and pants, make up puzzles, play with toy fire engines, and just run around like a maniac. There is also a dormitory up there and displays of fire-related toys and fire hats from around the world. This museum is only going to improve and become as popular as it deserves to be.

**RATING**

**ADDRESS/PHONE/WEB SITE**
1355 North Cahuenga Boulevard
Hollywood 90028
323-464-2727
www.lafd.org/museum.htm

**COST**
Free (nominal donations requested)

**PARKING**
Free

**HOURS**
Sat, 10:00 a.m.–4:00 p.m.

**STROLLER ACCESS**
Adequate for up to a double-wide stroller

**MORE THAN ONE ADULT NEEDED?**
No

**THE LOWDOWN**
Make sure you go upstairs!

## *...les Live Steamers Railroad Museum*

...yet another Griffith Park gem, and it's *free*! They run miniature train rides from 11:00 a.m.–3:00 p.m. every Sunday. However, there is a proviso: unless your children are at least thirty-four inches tall, they won't be able to ride. So unless you want to hold the screaming baby while others ride, make sure everyone in your party is tall enough to ride.

**RATING (IF EVERYONE'S OVER 34" TALL)**

**ADDRESS/PHONE/WEB SITE**

5202 Zoo Drive
Los Angeles 90027
323-662-5874

**COST**

Free

**PARKING**

Free

**HOURS**

Open Sunday, 11:00–3:00 (between Memorial Day weekend and the first Sunday in October)

**STROLLER ACCESS**

You'll be parking it and holding the kids in line, so it may be better to leave it in the car

**MORE THAN ONE ADULT NEEDED?**

No

**THE LOWDOWN**

There can be long lines for the rides, but it's free—what do you have to lose?

## Los Angeles Zoo

Everyone I know has a yearly membership to the zoo, yet no one I know wants to go. Why not? Kids love zoos, and it's free after you buy the membership, so why not go every week? Because of one major flaw: the Los Angeles Zoo is the only place on earth where everything is uphill. Somehow the zoo was constructed in a quantum universe where everything you want to see is uphill from where you are, yet when you leave you have to climb again.

The exact mechanics of this can't be explained by myself, my friends, or a physics professor. Even to get to the shuttle that relieves you of some of the walking, you have to scale a considerable hill—and then lug your children and stroller on and off the shuttle repeatedly, uphill every time.

The zoo itself, apart from this strange phenomenon, is quite pleasant. They are trying very hard to expand and improve the facilities for the animals. The new exhibits are really great, from the Children's Zoo as you enter (only a small hike uphill from the ticket booth to this one) to the Red Ape Rainforest (just uphill from the koalas). They are building more new exhibits down at the car park

**RATING**

**ADDRESS/PHONE/WEB SITE**

5333 Zoo Drive
Los Angeles 90027
323-666-4650
www.lazoo.org

**COST**

Adults (over 13), $10; seniors, $7; children 2–12, $5; under 2, free; shuttle bus: adults, $4; seniors, $1.50; children, $2; annual family pass, $65

**PARKING**

Free

**HOURS**

Open daily, 10:00 a.m.–5:00 p.m.; extended to 6:00 p.m. July 1–Labor Day; closed Christmas

**STROLLER ACCESS**

Take a jogger stroller; it's that much easier to push uphill

**MORE THAN ONE ADULT NEEDED?**

No

**THE LOWDOWN**

Go early in the day; it's the only way to beat the heat. If you go late in the afternoon, the animals have all been put to bed. Take good shoes and lots of water. There are healthy snacks for sale, but avoid the eating areas; we've found that the trash cans and food areas are often infested with wasps. You'll want to eat as far from the wasps as you can.

level, and I am looking forward to these as they may actually be on level ground. The middle of the zoo is also under construction, so right now you walk for a long time and see nothing, but soon (in 2005) this construction should be finished.

I am hoping that sometime soon they will give the polar bear a new home. Every time I see him hiding in his cave, sitting in front of the air conditioner, I feel so sorry for him that I want to start a "free the artic animals" campaign. And you will begin to know exactly how he feels, because after walking what seems like five hundred miles— uphill—all you'll want to do is prostrate yourself in front of refrigerated air. Instead you'll find yourself struggling to keep up with your two-year-old who, energized from her long ride, has now climbed out of the stroller and is chasing squirrels and pigeons with squeals of delight.

At the end of the day it won't be the great bird show you managed to catch after climbing to the top of the zoo or even the trained seals that your four-year-old will talk about on the way home—it'll be that funny squirrel who was chasing that other squirrel, you know, the one with the white butt.

## Lummis House and Gardens

Lummis House was built by Charles Lummis, the founder of the Southwest Museum. It is located immediately below the **Southwest Museum.** It features a house built of local materials and a garden suited to the desert climate. It should be a nice place to have a picnic, except that the house has an abandoned, haunted quality, and neither my daughter nor I felt at ease there. Skip this one and go straight to the Southwest Museum; there are picnic tables up there, and you'll have a great view.

**RATING**

**ADDRESS/PHONE/WEB SITE**
200 South Avenue 43
Highland Park 90042
323-222-0546

**COST**
Free

**PARKING**
Free

**HOURS**
Fri–Sun, 12:00–4:00 p.m.

**STROLLER ACCESS**
Good for up to a double-wide stroller; most of the paths are paved

**MORE THAN ONE ADULT NEEDED?**
No

**THE LOWDOWN**
If you want to find some great water-saving plants for your garden, take a trip here on your own.

# Museum of the American West

The Museum of the American West was formerly called the Gene Autry Museum, which is still what the signs on the freeway say. The place was named after a singing cowboy movie hero from a time when being a singing cowboy was cool. Gene Autry's legacy is an eclectic and entertaining collection of western art, movie memorabilia, and historical artifacts. The top floor contains changing exhibits. I love that even these temporary exhibits usually include hands-on areas for kids. One of the latest exhibits even had a replica of an 1830s Mexican American living area, where the kids could cook plastic tortillas in the fireplace and try to spin real wool. In addition, there were small children's reading areas and antique toys to play with.

**RATING**

**ADDRESS/PHONE/WEB SITE**
Griffith Park
4700 Western Heritage Way
Los Angeles 90027
323-667-2000

**COST**
Adults, $7.50; students and seniors, $5; children age 2–12, $3; free Thursday 4:00 p.m.–8:00 p.m.

**PARKING**
Free

**HOURS**
Tue–Sun, 10:00 a.m.–5:00 p.m.; extended to 8:00 p.m. on Thursday; closed New Year's Day, Thanksgiving, and Christmas

**STROLLER ACCESS**
Adequate for a double wide-stroller

**MORE THAN ONE ADULT NEEDED?**
No

**THE LOWDOWN**
This is a must-see museum!

Downstairs in the permanent exhibits, the tradition of immersion in culture and history is continued. In the McCormick Tribune Foundation Family Discovery Gallery, a house belonging to a Chinese family from the 1930s has been reconstructed, as well as the showroom of the family's import business and their Chinese restaurant. Even if your children are too young to observe that the pretend living room has no TV, they are plenty old enough to play with the old wooden blocks or pull the plastic food in and out of the antique oven and fridge. I usually get to sit down at the restaurant and be served plastic dim sum of astonishing variety.

You may never get to the rest of the museum, but if you do you'll find an astonishing collection of saddles, television and movie props, and short films pointing out the difference between the reality of the old West and Hollywood's portrayal of it. Make a special point to stop at the "blue screen horse." If you put your child on the horse's back, they can look at the television and see themselves riding off into the distance.

The museum is free on Thursday nights and virtually empty. I always go then, because my kids have a great time without having to fight for the toys in the Family Discovery Room. On a busy weekend I am sure it would not be as much fun, so get there between 4:00 p.m.–8:00 p.m. on Thursday and check it out. This is a way for your kids to learn about the history and varied culture of the region and, most of all, to have fun.

## Pony Rides and Southern Railroad

Here in Griffith Park is the place where most children in Los Angeles experience their first time on horseback. The pony rides are affordable and age suitable. For the very young there is a pony ring where the ponies walk while hitched to a turnstile. Once the kids are comfortable with this, they are ready for the slow ponies. These ponies walk twice around a large, oval track. Soon enough the kids will beg to go faster; the medium ponies trot for the first half of the track. And if your kids are too afraid of ponies to ride any of them, they can travel with you around the track in a mule-drawn wagon.

The only thing wrong with this is the wait time. Don't go on the weekend; the line is ridiculous. Also, if you think your children will want more than one ride, buy at least two tickets before they get on. If they want to go again, you just hand over another ticket; this way you don't have to stand in line again. My mom actually paid for my oldest to go around five times one day before she got bored, but hey, if a kid can't con her grandma. . . .

The Southern Railroad is the best way to bribe horse-loving girls to leave the ponies. It is a miniature railroad, and the conductors are generally fun and entertaining guys. The ride features a fake ghost town, a view of llamas and horses in pens, and concrete statuettes of Snow White and her dwarfs, and for little kids that is the best part of all.

**RATING**

**ADDRESS/PHONE/WEB SITE**
Griffith Park
Corner of Los Feliz and Riverside Drive
Hollywood 90027
323-664-3266 and 323-664-6788

**COST**
$2 to ride the ponies; $2 to ride the train; under 18 months, free

**PARKING**
Free

**HOURS**
Ponies: Tue–Sun, 10:00 a.m.– 4:00 p.m.; Train: Mon–Fri, 10:00 a.m.– 4:30 p.m; Sat–Sun, 10:00 a.m.– 5:00 p.m.

**STROLLER ACCESS**
Good for up to a double-wide stroller

**MORE THAN ONE ADULT NEEDED?**
No

**THE LOWDOWN**
Avoid going here on summer weekends; it's just too crowded.

## Ripley's Believe It or Not! Museum

There is something disturbing about the extremely odd, and Ripley's likes to play that up, taking the odd straight to the macabre. The television in the lobby hints at the delights within: A young man putting a snake up his nose and taking it out of his mouth, two-headed cows, and men impaled on metal stakes. All in all, the grotesque is the centerpiece of this "entertainment" experience.

I've never gone further than the lobby. This just seems like a remarkably inappropriate place to take any kid who is still young enough to believe in Santa. My kids have enough worries. Just the other day, my daughter was afraid that if she crossed her eyes they would stay that way; she doesn't need to see a pair of conjoined twins attached at the head. *Note:* There is another Ripley's museum in Buena Park. It's pretty much the same drill as this one.

**RATING**
0 strollers

**ADDRESS/PHONE/WEB SITE**
6780 Hollywood Boulevard (at Highland) Hollywood 90028
323-466-6335

**COST**
Adults (over 13), $10.95; children 6–12, $7.95

**PARKING**
$2 at Hollywood and Highland

**HOURS**
Open daily, 10:00 a.m.–10:00 p.m.

**STROLLER ACCESS**
Why would you take a stroller in here?

**MORE THAN ONE ADULT NEEDED?**
No

**THE LOWDOWN**
Just say no to grotesque entertainment.

# Southwest Museum

I have rarely been to a public place that is so poorly equipped for strollers or handicapped people. Unless you have a handicapped permit, there is a large flight of stairs from the parking to the entrance, and then there is no access from the top floor to the bottom floor without taking more stairs. There are even a couple of stairs to negotiate in order to get around the floor you are on. Don't let this keep you from going; just be aware that this is one of those places where you will be carrying the smaller kids. This is probably for the best anyway, as many of the exhibits that will interest the young ones are dioramas, built into the walls just above kid viewing range. My kids loved the displays, dioramas with small children in them, and clothing items that would fit them—ancient, kid-size moccasins and dresses—as well as Native American baby dolls. And if your kids want to know what a tipi is, there is a large, colorful one on display.

**RATING**

**ADDRESS/PHONE/WEB SITE**
234 Museum Drive
Los Angeles, CA 90065
323-221-2164

**COST**
Adults, $7.50; students and seniors (60+), $5; children 2–12, $3; Family pass for a year, $65, and this also works at the Museum of the American West

**PARKING**
Free; check out the easy access stroller parking spots

**HOURS**
Tue–Sun, 10:00 a.m.–5:00 p.m.; closed Thanksgiving and Christmas

**STROLLER ACCESS**
Inadequate

**MORE THAN ONE ADULT NEEDED?**
No

**THE LOWDOWN**
Take a stroller that you can easily carry up and down stairs.

Don't make the mistake of topping off this fun trip with a visit to the museum store. The items are largely of the breakable and expensive variety, so take the elevator down to the tunnel, which contains lots more dioramas. If your kids want more and are big enough for a hike, there is a garden and a steep set of steps (the Hopi Trail) down the hill.

# Summer Sounds Program at the Hollywood Bowl

You will hear great things about the Summer Sounds program at the Bowl. It is a program run in the summer for children. Here is the not so wonderful truth.

First, you won't be able to get tickets unless you buy them months in advance. The tickets are not cheap: $5 for a musical show lasting less than an hour and $3 for an arts and crafts area. Each child needs a ticket, and each parent must also purchase a ticket for the musical show. This makes for an expensive outing.

Be warned: you will spend the musical show sitting on the cement unless, unlike mine, your kids are willing to sit on the cement on their own while you warm a wooden bleacher behind them.

**RATING**

**ADDRESS/PHONE/WEB SITE**
2301 North Highland Avenue
Hollywood 90068
323-850-2000
www.hollywoodbowl.com

**COST**
$5 for the musical show and $3 for the arts and crafts area

**PARKING**
Free

**STROLLER ACCESS**
Adequate for a double-wide stroller

**MORE THAN ONE ADULT NEEDED?**
No

**THE LOWDOWN**
If your kids are under four, do something else. The shows can be a mixed bag. If you decide to go, book early, or it will be sold out.

The arts and crafts area was fun for all the kids. At least it was after I finally managed to find them a place to work and materials to use. When your kids finish one project, they can go to the next—where you have yet another opportunity to scrounge around for materials and a place for them to work.

Then the music show starts. There are two different shows each day, one aimed at younger kids and one at older ones. The Bowl recommended that I take my mixed-age group to the show for older kids. This turned out to be a mistake.

All of the shows are different. There were six shows last year, of which I only attended two. One was awful; it was dull, and the script talked down to the kids. The other show was fun and enjoyable. Of course the boring one was the first one we went to. I took four kids to the first show and was only able to drag two of them back to the second show, which made this an extremely expensive couple of days out.

Was it worth it? My daughter wants to see all six shows next summer, so I'll be back.

# Travel Town Museum

Travel Town is another of Griffith Park's wonders. For no admission fee you can take your kids in and they can climb up on and look at old trains. I should warn you that once you are up in the engine of these trains, you are up quite high, and you'll have to keep your eyes open to make sure that your little ones don't try to climb down on their own or just get scared. I would recommend taking another adult; one can climb up, and the kids can be passed to him/her, and vice versa when you disembark.

And then when that grows old, for a small fee you can take a miniature train around the museum and see all the trains again. Every time we go, the trains have been moved around, with different ones from different eras being restored and put on display. Inside the one large building there is a model train running behind a window made grubby by the eager kid noses constantly pushed against it. There is also a padded kids' area for playing—in addition to antique cars and other vehicles.

If you have active kids, I know this will turn into one of their favorite places.

**RATING**

**ADDRESS/PHONE/WEB SITE**
Griffith Park
5200 Zoo Drive
Los Angeles 90027
323-662-5874

**COST**
Free

**PARKING**
Free

**HOURS**
Mon–Fri, 10:00 a.m.–4:00 p.m., Sat–Sun, 10:00 a.m.–5:00 p.m.; closed Christmas

**STROLLER ACCESS**
Good with wide, paved paths for up to a double-wide stroller

**MORE THAN ONE ADULT NEEDED?**
Yes

**THE LOWDOWN**
If your kids love trains, it is also possible to have a birthday party here.

## Universal CityWalk

More than a shopping mall or an entrance to a theme park, Universal CityWalk has become an attraction in its own right. It's a place to go to walk, people watch, and play in the fountain or listen to street musicians.

CityWalk is busy and crowded on the weekends, especially during the summer, and can be a little hard to navigate with a large stroller, but it's worth the visit. Stop and eat, and just walk around people watching. Then, when your kids are bored with the stroller, let them play in the fountain, putting their hands in the steam coming off Universal's huge rotating globe statue, or watch the waves breaking again and again on the rocks outside the Billabong store.

CityWalk also features free

**RATING**

**ADDRESS/PHONE/WEB SITE**
Universal Studio Boulevard
818-622-4455
www.citywalkhollywood.com

**COST**
Free

**PARKING**
$10; or free if you take the Metro Red Line and catch the free shuttle up the hill

**HOURS**
Sun–Thu, 11:00 a.m.–9:00 p.m.; Fri–Sat, 11:00 a.m.–11:00 p.m.

**STROLLER ACCESS**
Easier with a single-wide stroller, particularly on the weekend

**MORE THAN ONE ADULT NEEDED?**
No

**THE LOWDOWN**
If you go in the evening, take a coat; the wind catches this hill.

outdoor films in the summer, live bands, and a small, outdoor ice skating rink in the winter.

To avoid the parking fee, catch the Metro Red Line, and walk across the street. There is a free shuttle that will take you up to CityWalk, and if it stops running before you head home, walking down the hill is fairly simple.

## Universal Studios

Universal Studios is my favorite amusement park. Does this mean it's a great place to take your kids? *No.* In fact, I find it to be less and less of a place to take young kids every time I visit.

Once upon a time, a long time ago, they used to make movies and give you a tour of the studio. The very fact that two hours of your day at this amusement park could be spent sitting down instead of walking in the insane heat was what I enjoyed about Universal. The problem is, they thought that just sitting on a bus and looking at sets was boring, so they started to add thrills. The studio tour now includes Jaws, an encounter with King Kong, and an earthquake. Jaws probably won't scare most kids, as long as they are warned ahead of time what to expect; King Kong will thrill a certain percentage of four-year-olds and scare the rest; but the earthquake will pretty much traumatize any toddler growing up in L.A. who has done an earthquake drill in preschool. If your kid is two or under, however, you can schedule the studio tour during what will be their normal naptime and they

**RATING**

**ADDRESS/PHONE/WEB SITE**
100 Universal City Plaza
Universal City 91608
1-800-UNIVERSAL
www.universalstudioshollywood.com

**COST**
Tickets start at about $39. At Universal they believe the rich are better, so if you pay more you can cut in line (in the summer the lines are very long, so be warned). Restricted Annual Passes tend to be fairly reasonable compared to the daily rate, and special deals are offered if you buy your tickets on-line, so check out www.universalstudioshollywood.com

**PARKING**
$10 (and I thought it was ridiculous at $7); or take the Metro Red Line and walk across the street—there is a free shuttle up the hill

**HOURS**
The hours vary from 9:00 a.m.–9:00 p.m. on weekends in the summer down to 10:00 a.m.–6:00 p.m. on winter days, so check the Web or call first

**STROLLER ACCESS**
Inadequate; to get from the top level to the bottom you have to either unload all the kids from the stroller and take the escalator or you have to take the elevator down one floor, then wait forever for a shuttle to take you down to the level below

**MORE THAN ONE ADULT NEEDED?**
Yes; a minimum of two if anyone wants to go on a ride

**THE LOWDOWN**
Wait until the kids are older unless you only go to the animal show and play area.

will quite happily sleep on your lap for two hours while you get to sit. So consider your kids' ages. If your preschoolers will be awake, this isn't the trip for them.

There is a kids' area where they can get wet or have balls lobbed at their heads. There is also a small playground. This area is best enjoyed when the park is empty, the weather's warm, and you've brought a change of clothes. The park, however, thinks that everything is best done at maximum volume, and I am sure that spending two entire days at the park will cause permanent hearing loss in most children. Even walking between rides you'll find yourself screaming, just so your kid in the stroller can hear you. It seems that every time I go there, they have turned the music and the general noise level up, and I just don't know why. The rest of the rides are largely aimed at older kids and adults. This is not a toddler park.

The only thing your little kids will definitely enjoy is the Animal Planet Show. This is a great show. I live only a few minutes from the park, and for a year we had an annual pass. We never went on a ride, but when my oldest was three we must have attended the Animal Planet Show twenty times.

The musical shows have, on the whole, been fun family entertainment, and the *Spiderman* musical is fun, but you should be aware there will be some explosions. The *Shrek 4D* movie is good, but again not necessarily good for younger kids. The rest of the shows are pretty much adult-only and tend to be loud and scary with explosions and violence.

I still love Universal Studios, but the next time I go I think I'll leave my kids home with my mom.

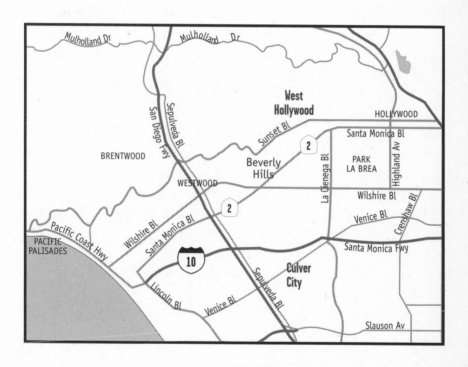

# The Westside

# Craft and Folk Art Museum

Instead of being a museum, this is an art gallery—a small art gallery. I am not sure what I was expecting, but it wasn't a gallery where kids can't touch and parents have to keep the stroller moving fast. The gift shop below was far more fascinating for my kids—and more expensive for me.

**RATING**

**ADDRESS/PHONE/WEB SITE**

5814 Wilshire Boulevard
Los Angeles 90036
323-937-4230
www.cafam.org

**COST**

Adults, $3.50; students/seniors, $2.50; children 12 and under, free; free admission on the first Wednesday of every month

**PARKING**

Available at meters on nearby streets or at one of the parking lots for the La Brea Tar Pits

**HOURS**

Wed–Sun, 11:00 a.m.–5:00 p.m.

**STROLLER ACCESS**

Adequate for any size stroller, single or double

**MORE THAN ONE ADULT NEEDED?**

No

**THE LOWDOWN**

Catch the gift shop and save the admission price of the galleries. If you really want to see and be able to appreciate the art, your best bet is a babysitter.

# Franklin Canyon

Hidden at the intersection of Coldwater Canyon and Mulholland Drive, on the ridge of the Santa Monica Mountains, lies this beautiful piece of wilderness. Once you've actually found it you'll never believe you are still in Los Angeles, let alone that the center of the city lies within the park.

As well as the large Franklin Canyon Lake, there is the smaller Heavenly Pond. This is fully accessible, with a wide paved path around the "duck pond." Many of the other paths in the park are accessible by jogger stroller if it hasn't been raining—and if you have assistance to get the stroller up and down some of the steps on these paths.

**RATING**

**ADDRESS/PHONE/WEB SITE**
2600 Franklin Canyon Drive
Beverly Hills 90210
310-858-3834

**COST**
Free

**PARKING**
Free

**HOURS**
Sunrise to sunset; the nature center is open 10:00 a.m.–4:00 p.m.; closed holidays

**STROLLER ACCESS**
Varies from perfect to lift and carry

**MORE THAN ONE ADULT NEEDED?**
No

**THE LOWDOWN**
It's hard to find; turn west on Franklin Canyon when you see the Mulholland Road sign (Tree People is across the street) and follow the sign that says Dead End. I think the locals know how great this spot is and don't want it full of people.

59

## The Getty Center

If you haven't yet visited the Getty with your child, don't. It is one of the least child-friendly places I have been. Unless your babies are young enough that they will stay willingly in the stroller and be quiet, this is not the place for them.

When I went with my three-year-old, she wanted to see everything. This was fine for some of the paintings, but she got bored. Then we came to the Ancient Greece exhibit. She just couldn't see from her knee-high perspective, so I lifted her out of the stroller. This was when the staff started screaming at me, "Don't let her touch anything!" As if I would. They also, unbelievably, wouldn't let me carry her, "for her own safety."

So I let her walk, and before she had taken two steps another security person told me, "She must be in her stroller; these are precious works of art." No kidding.

**RATING**

**ADDRESS/PHONE/WEB SITE**
1200 Getty Center Drive
Los Angeles 90049
310-440-7300

**COST**
Free

**PARKING**
$7

**HOURS**
Sun, Tue–Thu, 10:00 a.m.–6:00 p.m.; Fri–Sat, 10:00 a.m.–6:00 p.m.; closed Mondays, New Year's Day, Fourth of July, Thanksgiving, and Christmas

**STROLLER ACCESS**
Adequate for a double-wide strollers

**MORE THAN ONE ADULT NEEDED?**
Yes

**THE LOWDOWN**
The Getty is simply not geared toward young kids. Wait until they are school age. Or if you go, don't go alone; have at least two adults so that one of you can stick to the garden with the kids.

Later, we went out into the courtyard. The courtyard is beautiful; all of the buildings are arranged around a shallow, child-attracting, deathtrap of a fountain. Anywhere else an unfenced pool would be a hazard, but it's OK here, because the Getty has employed countless security guards who constantly tell you to keep an eye on your child. Imagine—you have to watch your children around water. Now there's a lesson I needed.

Then there are the tours of the garden and architecture. The only thing I learned on the architectural tour was that my three-year-old was not going to listen to someone talk endlessly about building foundations. She was understandably bored, and the stairs (large, steep, concrete), which she could climb down at a lightning pace, were the only piece of architecture she wanted to explore. The entire group walked away without us, and it took me twenty minutes to find the rest of my family.

The Getty does have a great garden, and if your child will keep off the plants and out of the stream it can be lots of fun. If you are determined to go to the Getty, keep your kids outside in the garden. Have at least one extra adult along, and take turns, with one of you going to see the art while the other plays chase on the grass.

There is a family room, and they say that on the weekends they have great things for kids, but I refuse to go back to find out. This may be one of the world's greatest museums, but there are so many other places in L.A. that are kid friendly I haven't bothered giving the Getty a second chance.

# The Grove/Los Angeles Farmers Market

This is a juxtaposition of two extremes. The Farmers Market has been around since 1934, and although it started as a farmers' market, it is now a conglomeration of little eating establishments with the occasional fruit stand. Most of the food is great—not that I've eaten everywhere, but everywhere I've eaten has been cheap and good. Also, this is kid friendly eating, out in the open air between stands. If your youngest runs around, no one will freak out; also, you can buy everyone in your party a completely different meal. And after you have eaten and checked out the hot sauce stand and the sticker stand, it's time to take on The Grove.

The Grove is a spanking new outdoor shopping mall, as posh as the Farmers Market is rickety. It's a nice place to stroll around, with little things that make it a place your kids will enjoy. There is an electric trolley that gives free rides up and down to the Farmers Market. The dancing fountains are beautiful, especially in darkness, and during the Christmas season this is one of the best places to come see Santa—not necessarily because of Santa, but because there is snowfall on the hour. From the buildings, they shoot peppermint-scented foam bubbles that float around and then disappear on the

**RATING**

**ADDRESS/PHONE/WEB SITE**

Third Street between Fairfax and LaBrea
Los Angeles 90036
Grove, 888-315-8883; Farmers Market, 323-933-9211
www.thegrovela.com

**COST**

Free

**PARKING**

Free if you park in the Farmers Market (not the Grove) and get validation; in the huge multi-story parking structure for the Grove the first hour is free, but few stores validate (the movies will not validate!), and the maximum charge is $12

**HOURS**

Approx. 9:00 a.m.–9:00 p.m.; the different stands and stores keep different hours

**STROLLER ACCESS**

Adequate for up to a double-wide jogger stroller

**MORE THAN ONE ADULT NEEDED?**

No

**THE LOWDOWN**

Park at the Farmers Market lot (on Fairfax), and get validation when you buy some food.

ground, and it's all choreographed to music. The tallest Christmas tree in Los Angeles is also at the Grove.

There is also a Kid's Club at the Grove. They have storytelling and other fun activities, summer through October, every Thursday. Check the Web site for details. In addition, the Grove has an overpriced movie theater and many of the nicer chain stores.

# La Brea Tar Pits/George Page Museum

This is a great way to spend an afternoon. The tar pits are set in a park and can be seen for free. Pit 91 is being excavated during the summer, and as long as your toddler isn't screaming "I need to pee!" (as mine was) you will be able to hear the docent, who is often on site during the digging, tell you what you are looking at. The tar pits themselves are nothing, however, if you don't go to the museum. My daughter asked me what the big deal was about the stinky lakes, and until we went into the museum I was actually hard-pressed to answer her.

Inside the museum you will find skeletons: lots and lots of remains of large, extinct animals. The mammoth skeleton is astonishing and even a little scary. And the tar in a jar demonstration, where the kids try to pull a metal rod out of sticky tar, is a great hands-on learning tool. They also get to see paleontologists at work in the fishbowl-style laboratory. This dull, boring work may put your child off dinosaurs forever, so don't linger.

**RATING**

**ADDRESS/PHONE/WEB SITE**

5801 Wilshire Boulevard
Los Angeles 90036
323-934-PAGE
www.tarpits.org

**COST**

Adults, $7; seniors (62+) and students with I.D., $4.50; children 5–12, $2; admission is free the first Tuesday of every month

**HOURS**

Mon–Fri, 9:30 a.m.–5:00 p.m.; Sat–Sun and holidays, 10:00 a.m.–5:00 p.m.; closed New Year's Day, Fourth of July, Thanksgiving, and Christmas

**PARKING**

$6 with museum validation in the parking lot behind the museum, but metered parking is also available on Sixth Street

**STROLLER ACCESS**

Good with wide aisles for up to a double-wide stroller

**MORE THAN ONE ADULT NEEDED?**

No

**THE LOWDOWN**

To save some money, you may want to catch the museum on their free Tuesday; or better yet, buy an annual pass, which will also give you admission to the Natural History Museum.

There are two films you can watch. The first, "Treasures of the La Brea Tar Pits," gives you the basic science, but is showing its age badly and is a very long ten minutes. The second, "Behind the Scenes," is very well done and modern, although by the time you get to it your kids may already have had enough (mine were finished and just wanted to go see the big "elephants" outside in the lake again).

On the way out, the kids can look at all the pits again with new appreciation and will have fun climbing on the concrete animals (ancient sloths). You will be on your way back home in about two hours.

## Los Angeles County Museum of Art (LACMA)

LACMA is an odd collection of buildings located on and near Hancock Park. The one specifically geared to children is actually a little removed from the rest, on the corner of Fairfax. It looks like an abandoned Macy's, which at some point it probably was. This building (LACMA West, which contains the Boone Children's Gallery), is the kids' art gallery where the art is interactive. Kids can create their own masterpieces with various supplies, from paint to glue and colored paper. Your children can make a great big creative mess—and it's free!

On most Sundays, LACMA West hosts Family Day, where even more crafts and art options are open to the kids, and once again, it's free! This is the best deal in town. Seriously, I hate to think what it costs them to keep this running when I see how much paint and glue my own kids are using on their art projects—and on their clothes.

**RATING**

**ADDRESS/PHONE/WEB SITE**

5905 Wilshire Boulevard
Los Angeles 90036
323-857-6000
www.lacma.org

**COST**

Free after your kids become NEXGEN members

**PARKING**

Up to $8, but you can usually find metered parking on Sixth Street

**HOURS**

LACMA West (kids' gallery): Mon–Tue, Thu–Fri, 12:00–5:00 p.m.; Sat–Sun, 11:00 a.m.–5:00 p.m.; LACMA East: Mon, Tue, Thu, 12:00–8:00 p.m.; Fri, 12:00–9:00 p.m.; Sat–Sun, 11:00 a.m.–8:00 p.m.; closed Wednesdays, Thanksgiving, and Christmas

**STROLLER ACCESS**

Adequate if you can find the elevators

**MORE THAN ONE ADULT NEEDED?**

No

**THE LOWDOWN**

Take your kids to the Family Sundays as often as possible.

LACMA East, located in Hancock Park, is modern, yet strangely stroller unfriendly. If you take a wrong turn, or want to look at the sculpture garden, or just walk to LACMA West, you find yourself facing stairs. Yes, there are elevators somewhere (I am told the elevator is located immediately inside the Wilshire Boulevard entrance of LACMA East), but I always seem to end up climbing down carrying the stroller.

LACMA East is a collection of different buildings, and different tickets are required to enter those different buildings. The ticket booth is located in the center of the courtyard, and the entire place is organized like a crossword puzzle without clues. However, sign your kids up for a NEXGEN membership. The helpful people at LACMA West will get you organized; now your kids get in free to all standard exhibits. They will even get a pretty membership card, and because you are with them you get in free, too.

LACMA is really trying to reach out to kids, and it shows. Take your kids, and if they get bored with painting or looking at art, let them run around Hancock Park a few times before you drive home.

## Museum of Jurassic Technology

This museum sounded like fun, maybe a tongue-in-cheek look at history, and I was looking forward to it. When you first come to the building, it appears shut and locked, and you have to ring the bell to get the door open. Once you enter, you leave all light behind. This museum is dark; a bat would feel right at home.

My five-year-old, who won't sleep without a nightlight, was not impressed, and we left shortly after arriving.

The exhibits are largely of the "read the card and stare at the lighted object" variety. All in all, if you want to go, leave the kids behind; this just isn't for them.

**RATING**

**ADDRESS/PHONE/WEB SITE**

9341 Venice Boulevard
Culver City 90232
310-836-6131
www.mjt.org

**COST**

Adults, $5; children 12–21, students with ID, and seniors (60+), $3; children under 12, free

**PARKING**

Free on surrounding roads

**HOURS**

Thu, 2:00 p.m.–8:00 p.m.; Fri–Sun, 12:00–6:00 p.m.; closed on Thanksgiving, Christmas, and the first Thursday in May

**STROLLER ACCESS**

Dangerous, not because there isn't clearance, but because you simply can't see where to go

**MORE THAN ONE ADULT NEEDED?**

No

**THE LOWDOWN**

Forget it.

## Museum of Television and Radio

I used to think of museums as places to go to get my kids away from just sitting down and watching TV. Then we visited this museum.

The museum's mission is to preserve television footage and radio broadcasts. Classic television shows are shown daily on large screens, and in the morning they generally play child-friendly shows. If you can't find something you love on one of the four big screens, you can visit the library upstairs. Here you can watch, for up to two hours, anything out of their catalogue of over a hundred thousand shows. There are seating areas that can hold up to three viewers at the same time. I was astonished and disgusted to see how entertained both my kids were by an old *Scooby Doo* episode. My five-year-old managed to get the computer to work, and I watched an entire sitcom without being interrupted—that never happens at home.

**RATING**

**ADDRESS/PHONE/WEB SITE**
465 North Beverly Drive
Beverly Hills 90210
310-786-1000
www.mtr.org

**COST**
Free—suggested donations of $10 for adults and $5 for children

**PARKING**
Free for first 2 hours

**HOURS**
Wed–Sun, 12:00–5:00 p.m.

**STROLLER ACCESS**
Adequate for up to a double-wide stroller

**MORE THAN ONE ADULT NEEDED?**
No

**THE LOWDOWN**
If you can't get the computer to run the TV show you want to watch, just ask any kid over three to help you.

# Petersen Automotive Museum

At $10 for adults and $6 for parking, the Petersen is one of the more expensive little museums in town, which is the main reason that I refused to take my oldest daughter back, although she wanted to go. It's not that she's a big fan of cars—she never plays with any of the toy cars she owns. She just liked the colors and thought the cars were pretty.

So even if your child is a girly-girl like mine and thinks that cars are boy stuff, this museum may hold her attention. And if you've got a car-loving boy, well, this place is heaven. Some of these cars are simply beautiful works of art. Which is the biggest problem with taking toddlers to this museum. The first two floors are strictly "look but don't touch." There is nothing at all hands-on about the experience. Even the Hotwheels exhibit has no child-friendly features. Children's toy cars are shown alongside life-size cars, yet nowhere are the kids allowed to touch either a toy or real car. It would have been nice.

The bottom floor is set up as a street scene of L.A. through the ages. I enjoyed it, but my oldest thought the "fake" people in the scenes were scary. The second floor was more to everyone's liking, except for the cars of celebrities. I mean, kids just don't get it. My

**RATING**

**ADDRESS/PHONE/WEB SITE**
6060 Wilshire Boulevard (at Fairfax)
Los Angeles 90036
323-930-CARS
www.petersen.org

**COST**
Adults (13+), $10; seniors (62+) and students, $5; children 5–12, $3; children under 5, free

**PARKING**
$6, but you can find cheaper metered parking

**HOURS**
Tue–Sun, 10:00 a.m.–6:00 p.m.; closed Mondays, New Year's Day, Thanksgiving, and Christmas

**STROLLER ACCESS**
Good for up to a double-wide stroller, with plenty of elevators

**MORE THAN ONE ADULT NEEDED?**
No

**THE LOWDOWN**
Don't take kids who are at that "touch everything" stage. (What's that, about one to fifteen?) The cars are pretty, but you are going to have to hustle to keep the kids from wanting to climb over the little ropes. This is a better museum for the other kid in your life, your husband.

daughter doesn't like a car because Nicolas Cage used to own it—she likes it because it's the same sparkly purple color as her new swimsuit.

The top floor is the Discovery Room area. And there we found the one car the kids are allowed to touch, a Model T Ford. My twenty-month-old loved it. She likes to pretend she can drive at every opportunity, and this was her one opportunity in the entire museum. The toddler area consists of road track rugs and toy cars and signs. The rest of the Discovery Room area is largely aimed at older children. The Petersen is trying, but compared to the Discovery Rooms at other museums or even an afternoon at Travel Town, this was disappointing. Travel Town actually lets the kids touch most of the exhibits, and it's free.

The fourth floor of the Petersen apparently shows cars being renovated. This is by appointment only, and I don't imagine that it would be preschool appropriate. If you love cars, by all means go to the museum, but don't expect it to be your kids' favorite place.

## Plummer Regional City Park

Nestled in West L.A. between apartment buildings is this strange "out of L.A." experience. All of a sudden you are transported to Europe, where old men sit around tables playing chess and talking with their hands while pigeons peck the ground. This multicultural park has all the amenities your kids will want: a great play area, room to run, shade, and restrooms. For the adults there are tennis courts, parking, and on Saturdays a farmers' market.

**RATING**

**ADDRESS/PHONE/WEB SITE**
7377 Santa Monica Boulevard
West Hollywood 90046

**COST**
Free

**PARKING**
Free

**HOURS**
Open daily dawn to dusk

**STROLLER ACCESS**
Good for up to a double-wide stroller

**MORE THAN ONE ADULT NEEDED?**
No

**THE LOWDOWN**
If you live close by, you'll love this park.

# Star Eco Station

Nestled in amongst commercial warehouses is this camouflage netting-covered building. It should stand out, yet I managed to drive past it three times. There's a big sign too, so I have no excuse, and you'll probably find it with little trouble. Anyway, the Star Eco Station is a wildlife rescue facility. The only way to see what they do is to take the tour. Tours run on the hour, and although I generally avoid them like the plague (nothing like chasing a two-year-old through areas you aren't supposed to be in), this tour was amazing. The guide kept the entire talk entertaining and easy enough for the kids to understand. We visited the fish room, the reptile room, and the bird room. In each room the guide explained why the animals were there, why they weren't great pets (did you know a parrot

**RATING**

🚼🚼🚼🚼🚼

**ADDRESS/PHONE/WEB SITE**

10101 West Jefferson Boulevard
Culver City 90232
310-824-8060
www.ecostation.org

**COST**

Adults, $7; seniors, $6; children age 2–12, $5

**PARKING**

Free in their lot in the rear of the building

**HOURS**

Mon–Fri, 9:00 a.m.–3:00 p.m.;
Sat, 10:00 a.m.–4:00 p.m.

**STROLLER ACCESS**

Adequate for either a single or double wide, although if you are part of a big tour the larger stroller may be a nuisance

**MORE THAN ONE ADULT NEEDED?**

No

**THE LOWDOWN**

Take your kids now! We loved this place and want to go back soon.

can live 150 years and will pull all its feathers out if it doesn't get enough attention?), and what needed to be done to protect them. There was a model of the stormwater system and an explanation of what happens when waste goes into the ocean (this is useful information for any age). The highlight of the trip was the room that contained not only a stuffed leopard (seized from a lawyer's office—yes, some of the jokes are true) but also two big cats (quite alive and walking around) that had been pets.

When my youngest got a little antsy, I was able to take her back to the animals we had just seen, but all in all the tour was fast-moving and entertaining throughout. At the end of the tour we all got to touch a gecko lizard. This was a great hour-long trip and a wonderful visit for any age. (They also host birthday parties.)

# Zimmer Children's Museum

This is one of the best places in L.A. to take your kids. And no one knows about it. It's located in the Jewish Federation Building, and although you will have to go through metal detectors to get in, once you are actually within the museum it is wonderful.

The top floor of this little museum contains a plane where your fledgling pilots can pretend to actually fly, dressed up in real, adult-sized uniforms. Or perhaps they would prefer to hold little flags and wear an orange hat as part of the ground crew. And in two minutes, when your kids are done with this and have stamped their new paper passport with four locations, they can head to the stage behind the admission desk. There they will find enough costumes to outfit an entire opera company, and a stage on which they can perform—complete with changeable backdrops and a closed circuit camera for viewing their own perfomance.

**RATING**

**ADDRESS/PHONE/WEB SITE**
The Goldsmith Jewish Federation Center
6505 Wilshire Boulevard, Suite 100
Los Angeles 90048
323-761-8989
www.zimmermuseum.org

**COST**
Adults, $5; children 3–12, $3; seniors and children under 3 free.

**PARKING**
Free

**HOURS**
Tue, 10:00 a.m.–5:00 p.m.; Wed–Thu, Sun, 12:30 p.m.–5:00 p.m.; closed Monday, Friday, Saturday, and on Jewish and national holidays

**STROLLER ACCESS**
Adequate, but don't bother; leave it in the car

**MORE THAN ONE ADULT NEEDED?**
No

**THE LOWDOWN**
If your kids love dress-up and pretend games, they will adore this place. Just make sure that it isn't a Jewish holiday on the day you go.

Downstairs is the largest part of the museum. With a stroller you'll have to go back through the inhospitable lobby, down the elevator, and through a hall. A better bet would be to leave your stroller upstairs or in the car. Just walk down the stairs. More kid-sized wonders await at an entire little village to pretend in: a store, restaurant, temple, house, and library, all equipped for imaginative play. My daughters spent twenty minutes in the restaurant alone, serving me plastic food which (though rather expensive) I was able to pay for with the toy money the Zimmer provided.

There is also a baby room with mirrors and foam to bounce around on (see if you can keep your five-year-old out of there—I couldn't). Then in the main room is another opportunity to pretend: an ambulance all ready to go, complete with uniforms and supplies, as well as an emergency room. As if these aren't enough, there are a few more treats, including a "river," where you are given obstacles and boats to run the courses you build, and computers that let you compose music with color.

If you go to this jewel of a place during the week, odds are you and your kids will be the only ones there. If you are accustomed to waiting in line and being in a crowd and would find this privacy creepy, bring a playgroup with you.

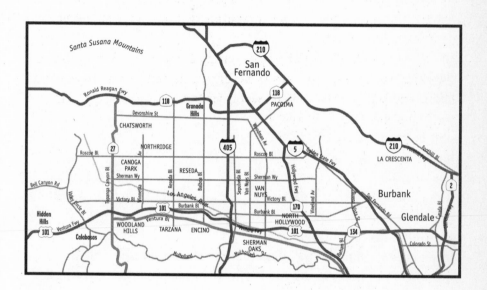

# San Fernando Valley
# ("The Valley")

## Chuck E. Cheese

There is a hell, and it's run by a giant rat. Chuck E. Cheese advertises constantly on PBS, and my oldest thought she would be going to paradise. When it turned out to be an overcrowded nightmare, she begged me to never take her there again.

Chuck E. Cheese has annoyingly (and possibly permanently damaging) loud music. The various games and play equipment are overcrowded and filled with bigger, more aggressive children. At least on the weekend, Chuck E. Cheese makes its money by scheduling enough birthday parties at the same time to not only turn each birthday celebration into a meaningless and rather pointless exercise in mass crass commercialism, but also to possibly break every fire code regarding capacity in Los Angeles.

If you still feel the need to go and play carnival-type games for three hours in order to earn your child a toy they could buy at the dollar store, then go on a weekday when at least you can actually find a machine to spend your money on.

**RATING**

**ADDRESS/PHONE/WEB SITE**
Numerous locations around Los Angeles
www.chuckecheese.com

**COST**
Incalculable

**PARKING**
Free

**HOURS**
Varies

**STROLLER ACCESS**
Little or none on weekends

**MORE THAN ONE ADULT NEEDED?**
No

**THE LOWDOWN**
Boycott all birthday parties being held here. Save yourself; you have been warned!

# Color Me Mine

Color Me Mine is a place where you can buy a piece of pottery that your child can paint; then it is fired, and you get to take home their creation. Sounds like a great idea, doesn't it? Well it is, except that it really doesn't work for pre-school kids. Come on, you've seen your kid paint: *splish, splash, splosh,* "Done, Mom!" So then they want another piece to paint on. On a per minute basis, this turns into incredibly expensive entertainment.

This chain has a great idea and it works well for older kids, but unless you have unlimited funds, wait until your kid is ready to paint and appreciate details.

**RATING**

**ADDRESS/PHONE/WEB SITE**
Various venues throughout Los Angeles
www.colormemine.com

**COST**
Incalculable

**PARKING**
Free

**HOURS**
Varies

**STROLLER ACCESS**
Depends upon location

**MORE THAN ONE ADULT NEEDED?**
No

**THE LOWDOWN**
Wait until your kid is a little older.

## Creative Leap

Creative Leap is another indoor playground. This one in North-ridge features a huge, McDon-ald's-style climbing structure as well as a rock climbing wall, a café (no outside food allowed), a huge ball pit, a building block pit, and a baby area. The baby area wasn't as much fun for my baby as the foam climbing moun-tain in the center of the room. While other parents were com-menting on how clean everything was (compared to Under the Sea and similar places), I was having a minor allergy attack from the inches of dust that coat the climbing structure (you never see that at McDonald's).

The climbing structure is a great place to lose older preschool-ers for a couple of hours, and if it's raining and wet and you live close, this is a fun way to spend the morning (it tends to get crowded in the afternoon).

**RATING**

**ADDRESS/PHONE/WEB SITE**
19300 Rinaldi Street, Unit M
Northridge 91326
818-366-3036

**COST**
$7 per child on weekdays, $8 per child on weekends

**PARKING**
Free

**HOURS**
Sun–Thu, 10:00 a.m.–6:00 p.m.; Fri–Sat, 10:00 a.m.–7:00 p.m.

**STROLLER ACCESS**
Adequate for up to a double-wide stroller

**MORE THAN ONE ADULT NEEDED?**
No

**THE LOWDOWN**
Bring socks and a couple of kids and just let them run in this safe, clean environment while you read a book.

## The Farm

I would never have believed a place like this could exist in Los Angeles. Set on a busy street is this oversized lot filled with animals. In fact, I have never seen so many animals crammed together in such close quarters outside of cattle feed lots. The most important thing to remember here is *don't buy animal food*! You will be attacked by the goats, pigs, chickens, and donkey if you are carrying food, and being nibbled by a goat is a little much for most adults, let alone kids.

Even if you don't buy food, this is going to be a close encounter of the animal kind. With the goats (the kids are soooo cute), sheep, pigs, bunnies, chickens, turkeys, ducks, geese, llamas, ostriches, donkey, and ponies, this is a petting zoo menagerie. My youngest, who was very timid around animals, decided to ride

**RATING**

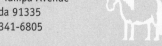

**ADDRESS/PHONE/WEB SITE**
8101 Tampa Avenue
Reseda 91335
818-341-6805

**COST**
General admission (over age one), $5; seniors, $2; pony rides, $3

**PARKING**
Free on nearby streets

**HOURS**
Sat–Sun, 10:00 a.m.–5:00 p.m.; open until 6:00 p.m. in the summer

**STROLLER ACCESS**
Leave the stroller at home

**MORE THAN ONE ADULT NEEDED?**
No

**THE LOWDOWN**
Wear rubber boots, and bring baby wipes and antibacterial gel to clean everyone's hands at the end. Don't buy any animal feed. There is poop everywhere; if you can't deal with that and the conditions the animals live in, don't go. By the time you pay for a couple of pony rides this is going to be an expensive outing.

her first pony after petting and chasing the goats. It was a great experience for her, and the older one loved it too. Personally, I just wish we had worn rubber boots because all those animals covered everything in a rich layer of manure.

# IKEA

When you go to IKEA for the first time, you realize how little most places care about customers with kids. With family parking right near the entrance and well-designed family restrooms, IKEA is the one place that has put real thought into what a parent needs. You can leave your bigger kids in the play area for older children. You will be given a pager so that you can go and shop for up to an hour, and if your kid has any problems, they will page you.

There is also an area where you can watch your babies play. I was there one afternoon sitting with my husband on a leather sofa, watching my kids swim in the ball pit, when he turned to me and said, "This is so much better than an amusement park. At an amusement park I never get to sit." A few minutes later a young mother came up to me and said, "You know, we went to Disneyland last week, and this is so much more fun."

IKEA is best visited during the week when it is not too busy. That way your kids can play on all the kids' furniture, although I will say that it is best if your children don't know you can buy any of the stuff they're playing on. And don't buy any furniture that you will have to wait to pick up. If you want to buy items you have to wait for, do it without the kids.

**RATING**

🪑🪑🪑🪑🪑

**ADDRESS/PHONE/WEB SITE**

600 N. San Fernando Boulevard
Burbank 91502
818-842-4532
20700 South Avalon Boulevard
Carson 90746
310-527-4532
848 South Barranca Avenue
Covina 91702
626-732-4532
1475 South Coast Drive
Santa Ana 92701
714-444-4532
www.ikea.com

**COST**

Free—although it's hard to get out of there without buying *something*

**PARKING**

Free, and check out the easy access stroller parking spots

**HOURS**

Open everyday, 10:00 a.m.–9:00 p.m.

**STROLLER ACCESS**

Adequate for a double-wide stroller

**MORE THAN ONE ADULT NEEDED?**

No

**THE LOWDOWN**

What are you waiting for? This is Disneyland for adults.

The restaurant serves cheap children's meals, and if you think the main bathroom with step stools for little kids to wash their hands, a diaper dispenser, and a bottle warming station is great, check out the family restroom. There you will find a comfortable chair for breastfeeding, a dollhouse for the little ones to play with, and a lower sink for the kids to wash their own hands. It's enough to make you wonder if you shouldn't move to Sweden. Or move to IKEA—they've got plenty of beds! *Note:* There are several IKEA locations in Southern California. They are virtually identical.

# Leonis Adobe Museum

Calabasas is trying to keep the feel of a small, western township while Los Angeles grows around it, and this little museum does its best to keep the past alive. Set right against the freeway, the Leonis Adobe was the home of one of the early Spanish ranchers in Los Angeles. Construction on the house was started in 1844, and it grew into a graceful, two-story home that has been preserved along with a small, Victorian cottage (the Plummer House). But it's not the restored, furnished houses that will excite your kids—it's everything else.

Outside the house they have preserved the idea of what life on a nineteenth-century rancho was like. There is an entire farmyard of animals: horses, ducks, turkeys, sheep, goats, and more. We were directed by the helpful staff to the barn, where we found a little lamb only a few weeks old and some young goat kids. There is a pump house and a water tower, as well as the original outhouses (clean, although my oldest still thought the entire idea was gross!). There is also a large display of farming equipment; you'll have to tell your kids to keep off of it. The highlight for us was the laundry facility. They have an entire laundry area set up outside, complete with hand wringers and washboards. I just wish my kids would be that interested in

**RATING**

**ADDRESS/PHONE/WEB SITE**
23537 Calabasas Road
Calabasas 91302
818-222-6511
www.leonisadobemuseum.org

**COST**
Donations of $4 per adult and 50 cents per child ages 2–12

**PARKING**
Free

**HOURS**
Wed–Sun, 1:00–4:00 p.m.; Sat 10:00 a.m.–4:00 p.m. and by special appointment

**STROLLER ACCESS**
Adequate for up to a double-wide stroller

**MORE THAN ONE ADULT NEEDED?**
No

**THE LOWDOWN**
Take a picnic lunch, and have lunch at the park before you go home.

helping do the laundry at home. As it was, everyone got wet and dirty washing the clothes that were supplied. It was great.

Before you go home, take a walk to the street corner, where the museum has established a gorgeous little park compete with a nineteenth-century rose garden and, more important to your kids, a small pond with a huge flock of ducks.

## Mission of San Fernando Rey de España

The seventeenth of the missions built in Los Angeles, this is a large complex of beautifully restored buildings dating back to 1797.

The church is a replica of the original and is an active church; the last time we were there it was all decorated for a wedding later in the day. Around the courtyard the smaller mission buildings are set up as exhibits showing early mission life. There is a weaving room, set up with a loom, and a blacksmith shop, pictures of Indian life, and clothing and artifacts. The mission has decided to protect its exhibits by putting up iron bars, which led my daughter to ask if this used to be a jail—I'm not sure she believed me when I said no.

**RATING**

**ADDRESS/PHONE/WEB SITE**
15151 San Fernando Mission Boulevard
Mission Hills 91345
818-361-0186

**COST**
Adults, $4; seniors and children 7–15, $3; children 6 and under, free

**PARKING**
Free

**HOURS**
Open daily, 9:00 a.m.–5:00 p.m.; closed Thanksgiving and Christmas

**STROLLER ACCESS**
Adequate for up to a double-wide stroller

**MORE THAN ONE ADULT NEEDED?**
No

**THE LOWDOWN**
Take your kids; they should know there was life before television.

Outside in the courtyard is a beautiful old fountain, which both of my kids wanted to watch. If you follow the map you will find the Hospice and Convento buildings and a ruined wall which shows how the adobe buildings were constructed. The Hospice and Convento are both restored and open to the public with displays of life in the nineteenth century, although these weren't as interesting to my kids as the workshop displays they had already seen.

## Sepulveda Dam Recreation Area—Balboa Park

Here in the center of the Valley is another huge city park with fun for everyone. The centerpiece of the park is Lake Balboa, where you can fish, rent a pedal boat, or find the remote-control model boating area and watch graceful, miniature boats sail and power about the water. There is also a model airplane field and a Japanese garden.

Our favorite, however, is the wilderness preserve, where you can take a paved path right out to a small lake. Great blue herons, snowy egrets, ducks, and pelicans can be seen there, along with many other birds. It's a lovely place to take a walk in the early evening, when the air is cooler and all the birds are returning to their roosts for the night. Hopefully, after running around madly, your kids will be ready to roost without a fuss, too.

**RATING**

**ADDRESS/PHONE/WEB SITE**
6335 Woodley Avenue
Van Nuys 91406-6473
818-756-8188

**COST**
Free

**PARKING**
Free

**HOURS**
Sunrise to sunset

**STROLLER ACCESS**
Great for up to a double-wide stroller

**MORE THAN ONE ADULT NEEDED?**
No

**THE LOWDOWN**
You can't feed the birds or take dogs into the wilderness preserve, but you can watch a heron catch his dinner, or a swallow nesting with only the sounds of birds and kids filling the air.

## Sheriff's Museum

This unadvertised, unmarked, virtually unvisited little museum is located in the Sheriff Training College. There is plenty of free parking, but you'll have to ask before you'll be able to find the building.

Inside you will find a CHP motorbike, which the kids can sit on. My two-year-old fell in love with the bike and then wanted to climb on everything in the museum, which, of course, is frowned upon. So my advice is to do the motorbike last. There is also a helicopter ("look, don't touch"), an "old West" jail, a 1930s police car, and a variety of uniforms and equipment on display. This is a small museum that won't take long to visit; it's also free. So if you are in the neighborhood, take a look.

**RATING**

**ADDRESS/PHONE/WEB SITE**
11515 South Colima Road
Whittier 90604
562-946-7081

**COST**
Free

**PARKING**
Free

**HOURS**
Mon–Fri, 9:00 a.m.–4:00 p.m.; closed holidays

**STROLLER ACCESS**
Adequate for up to a double-wide stroller

**MORE THAN ONE ADULT NEEDED?**
No

**THE LOWDOWN**
Take a camera; there's nothing cuter than a toddler wearing an oversized helmet on a huge motorbike.

## Sherman Oaks Castle Park

If your kids are past the stage of using a golf club as a weapon, here is a nice family outing. This city-run park contains batting cages, an arcade, and, best of all, three cute, eighteen-hole miniature golf courses. I'll admit that I'd rather go with my husband, because at least he doesn't cry if he loses (well, most of the time). But this is also a fun place for the kids, especially early on a weekend morning, when it is quite inexpensive.

**RATING**

**ADDRESS/PHONE/WEB SITE**
4989 Sepulveda Boulevard
Sherman Oaks 91403
818-756-9459
www.shermanoakscastle.com

**COST**
Miniature golf: Adults, $6.50; children under 12 and seniors, $5.50; replays and weekend mornings from 9:00 a.m.–10:30 a.m., $3

**PARKING**
Free

**HOURS**
Mon–Thu, 10:00 a.m.–11:00 p.m., Fri, 10:00 a.m.–midnight; Sat, 9:00 a.m.–midnight; Sun, 9:00 a.m.–11:00 p.m.

**STROLLER ACCESS**
Adequate for up to a double-wide stroller

**MORE THAN ONE ADULT NEEDED?**
Yes

**THE LOWDOWN**
Keep the kids out of the games arcade, or this will end up being a really expensive outing.

# Skirball Cultural Center

This large museum reminds me of the museums of my youth. There are plenty of interesting things to look at, most of which are safety tucked behind glass. The museum marks the history of the Jewish people (it does not, however, dwell on the Holocaust, nor are there any images displayed that would be inappropriate for kids).

One of the more interesting exhibits is a circular room with changing media images from the last century. Further into the museum is an exhibit devoted to American immigration, including a huge photograph of a ship arriving and a travel chest with kid-sized clothes that your children can try on. Now, this would have been our hands-down favorite thing in the whole place if only the security guard had not told us off for touching the clothes (he was quite put out when I showed him the sign that said "Please Try These On") and then yelled at us for taking a photo.

**RATING**

**ADDRESS/PHONE/WEB SITE**
Skirball Center Drive
Los Angeles 90025
310-440-4500
www.skirball.org

**COST**
Adults, $8; seniors and students, $6; children under 12, free; special exhibits are extra; free every Thursday

**PARKING**
Free

**HOURS**
Tue–Sat, 12:00–5:00 p.m.; Thu, 12:00–9:00 p.m., Sun, 11:00–5:00 p.m.; closed Mondays

**STROLLER ACCESS**
Good for up to a double-wide stroller

**MORE THAN ONE ADULT NEEDED?**
No

**THE LOWDOWN**
Try out one of their family oriented days and be on the lookout for authority-wielding idiots.

Around the corner was a room set up like a 1930s kitchen, with only a rail holding anyone back and a sign saying that alarms would go off if you leaned into the room. When my two-year-old wanted to climb into the room and play with the pots, I almost let her; it seemed like suitable payback for the guard.

The museum is trying to provide an educational family experience.

They have fun family-centered days for Jewish and American holidays, for which they have storytellers and arts and crafts. In addition they have children's programs, for toddlers on up. If they would only child-proof any attraction they don't want kids to play in and train their guards better, this would be a really fun place.

# Under the Sea

Under the Sea is a chain of indoor playgrounds. When the weather is just too wet or it's too hot to play outside, here is a place to go. Under the Sea is also a great place to have a birthday party. If you have a birthday at Under the Sea, you exclusively book out the entire venue for your party (unlike at Chuck E. Cheese or McDonald's).

The place is equipped with small climbing structures and slides, a bouncy house, pedal and push cars, and balls to play with. This is one of those occasions when you will have to play along with your smaller children, but it will be fun. If you take a small group, they will create their own games by chasing each other or racing pedal cars.

Everyone must wear socks, even the babies, but you are allowed to bring your own food in with you. Maintenance at these locations appears to be slacking off, and the toys aren't always as clean or operational as you might hope, but the kids have never noticed. We've always had fun here, and we are considering it for our next birthday party. (But I will be quite honest: if there's a nice McDonald's with a clean, uncrowded play area in your neighborhood, it is free and can be just as much fun.)

**RATING**

**ADDRESS/PHONE/WEB SITE**
20929 Ventura Boulevard
Woodland Hills 91364
818.999.1533
19620 Nordhoff Street
Northridge 91324
818.772.7003
2424 West Victory Boulevard
Burbank 91506
818.567.9945

**COST**
Children, $7; adults, free

**PARKING**
Free

**HOURS**
Mon–Fri, 10:00 a.m.–6:00 p.m.; parties held Sat–Sun

**STROLLER ACCESS**
Leave the stroller behind

**MORE THAN ONE ADULT NEEDED?**
No

**THE LOWDOWN**
Bring socks for *everyone,* including yourself and the baby—otherwise you will be buying overpriced, ill-fitting socks at their counter.

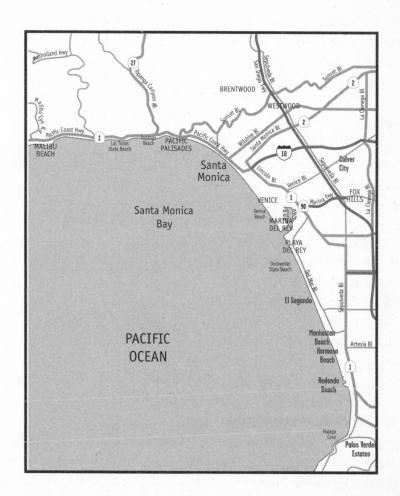

# Beaches

# Angels Attic

The idea of taking my two-year-old to this place didn't excite me. I dreaded the idea of her touching and breaking everything, but as it turned out my fears were unfounded. Set in a gorgeous Victorian house is this amazing collection of dolls, dollhouses, and miniatures, and it has been arranged practically and beautifully.

The dollhouses are (with the exception of one room) set behind glass, where they can be seen but not touched, and instead of the usual situation where you have to lift smaller children up so they can see, the displays are set from ground level up. In fact, my toddler pulled my hand and brought me down to her level so that I could enjoy some of the miniature delights she had found awaiting her.

**RATING**

**ADDRESS/PHONE/WEB SITE**
516 Colorado Avenue
Santa Monica 90401
310-394-8331

**COST**
Adults, $6.50; children under 12, $3.50; seniors (65+), $4

**PARKING**
Metered parking is available on the street

**HOURS**
Thu–Sun, 12:30–4:30 p.m.; closed New Year's Day, Easter, Fourth of July, Thanksgiving, Christmas Eve, and Christmas

**STROLLER ACCESS**
Inadequate; leave it behind

**MORE THAN ONE ADULT NEEDED?**
No

**THE LOWDOWN**
Be prepared to have your kids beg for the items at the bookstore.

The museum is not stroller friendly; even if you get through the first floor with a stroller, there is no elevator to the second floor. But your kids really shouldn't be in a stroller here, anyway. They should be allowed to explore and discover the charming little houses and rooms and scenes from yesteryear. Upstairs there is very little: one room with dolls and a sunny nook set up as a reading room and bookstore. Between the admission price and the bookstore, this turned out to be an expensive outing—but one we all enjoyed.

## California Heritage Museum

With such a prestigious name I expected more, and thus are all disappointments born. This house (and it's merely cute, turn of the century, beautifully preserved) is still just a house. To enter, one must take a tour. This is generally the kiss of death with young kids, but as it happened the docent who led us through the museum was wonderful. She really spoke *to* my children without talking down to them and showed us the Monterey furniture and the china on display. Then she took us up to the second floor, where their changing exhibits can be found.

Because of the nature of the museum—a "look don't touch" place with very little to catch a child's fancy—I would generally advise you to skip it. However, due to our lovely experience with this knowledgeable and helpful docent, I encourage you to go to the museum if the changing exhibit happens to be something that interests you. Check the Web site or call.

**RATING**

**ADDRESS/PHONE/WEB SITE**
2612 Main Street
Santa Monica 90405
310-392-8537
www.californiaheritagemuseum.org

**COST**
Free

**PARKING**
Free

**HOURS**
Wed–Sun, 11:00 a.m.–4:00 p.m.

**STROLLER ACCESS**
Inadequate; the second floor is not stroller accessible at all

**MORE THAN ONE ADULT NEEDED?**
No

**THE LOWDOWN**
If you have some time to kill in Santa Monica, and no expectations, this could be a short little visit.

## ... Creek Canyon

Because it's hidden away, you have probably driven past this park when you've gone to Mailbu. It is a beautiful park, deep into the Santa Monica Mountains; but what it is most famous for is being the site where the TV series *M*A*S*H* was filmed.

Start at the Visitors Center, which features a small museum including *M*A*S*H* memorabilia and stuffed animals, then cross the creek. When you come back, you may want to stop for a dip in the clean, clear water. The first part of the walk is shaded and gradually the grade increases until you get to the top of the hill, where Century Lake (a reservoir) awaits.

**RATING**

**ADDRESS/PHONE/WEB SITE**
Four miles south of Highway 101 on Las Virgenes/Malibu Canyon Road
818-880-0367

**COST**
Free

**PARKING**
Free

**HOURS**
Open every day, dawn to dusk

**STROLLER ACCESS**
Great for up to a double-wide stroller

**MORE THAN ONE ADULT NEEDED?**
No

**THE LOWDOWN**
Take water and sunscreen and enjoy nature.

You are now about halfway to the jeep that marks the site where *M*A*S*H* was filmed. It was at that point my kids wanted to go home. They'd walked uphill for a mile and the idea of going another mile was just too much. So take lots of water and a jogger stroller unless you want the trip to be cut short. The paths are level and wide and easily accessible. If you are lucky, you may even see a rattlesnake sunbathing, like we did.

# Redondo Beach and Pier

Redondo Beach is an easy beach to take the kids to. There is easy parking underneath the pier that is cheaper than parking at most beaches, especially for a short visit. The sand near the pier is coarser than Manhattan or Hermosa Beach. There is constant erosion here, and the beach is narrower in this area, but this actually makes it easier to get the stroller and kids from the walkway to the ocean.

The odd-looking pier (it's a three-legged affair where all the legs join at an angle in the entrance) offers a variety of shops and restaurants on the wide walkways. My kids loved the live crabs, fish, and lobsters on display at all the various restaurants, but I didn't bother informing them that these creatures were on the menu. Instead, we just had an ice cream and strolled on the pier.

**RATING**

**ADDRESS/PHONE/WEB SITE**
310-318-0631
www.redondopier.com

**COST**
Free

**PARKING**
1 hour free with validation Mon–Fri, otherwise at most $5 on weekdays in the summer and $7 on weekends in the summer

**STROLLER ACCESS**
Adequate for up to a double-wide jogger stroller

**MORE THAN ONE ADULT NEEDED?**
No

**THE LOWDOWN**
As with all Los Angeles beaches, it will be brutally cold in the winter and even chilly in the summer; don't rush down in the morning, let the fog burn off.

At one end is a bait shop where you can rent a fishing rod and buy bait, so if you want to take your kids fishing, here is an opportunity to do it without investing in any equipment (since most preschoolers think fishing is a great idea for about ten minutes). Then, when you get bored with that, you can walk around to the Shark Attack shop, which is shaped like a boat. If you purchase $5 worth of bric-a-brac for the kids, or spend $2 per adult and $1.50 per kid for tickets, you can all see a sixteen-foot stuffed great white shark. Honestly, it's not worth the money when you can see entire aquariums for free, but my daughter was proud of herself for not being scared of the shark (quite frankly, it looked fake behind its large window).

The pier also hosts special events like Fourth of July fireworks (spectacular—and crowded), a Halloween party, and Christmas Santas. The beach is also part of the amazing twenty-seven-mile bike trail that leads from Santa Monica to Torrance Beach. I know they weren't thinking of strollers when they built it, but it's a great walkway to take the kids along for plenty of fresh air and people watching. Remember to stay to the right and keep your kids close, as cyclists and skaters can zip past at great speed.

If you have some binoculars, bring them along because a group of sea lions has taken to sunbathing on a float in the small harbor. There is also a rock jetty with small creatures scurrying among the boulders, but it's a little dangerous for smaller children. Redondo is a great beach to keep everyone busy and entertained.

# Roundhouse Aquarium and Manhattan Beach

A lovely surprise lies at the end of the Manhattan Beach Pier. In a small building, which looks barely large enough for the café and restrooms it also holds, is the Roundhouse Aquarium. The first thing you will see when entering the aquarium are the touch tanks. These tanks are set up to be child friendly with extra stepstools provided to enable the little ones not only to look, but also to touch. From the tidepool touch tanks to the shark and ray touch tank, the kids will run about happily discovering even bigger tanks where larger rays, sharks, and a *huge* spiny lobster await.

Then the aquarium continues upstairs with a shell that was shed by the enormous lobster on the first floor and smaller tanks where the kids can see, among other creatures, an octopus and fish fetuses developing within their cases. Volunteers are ready and available to answer questions.

Manhattan Beach itself is a wide white beach with surf and standard Los Angeles freezing water. There is a strand running the length of the beach, making it easy to walk along with a stroller (provided, of course, you don't get run over by a bike or a skater).

**RATING**

**ADDRESS/PHONE/WEB SITE**
Manhattan Beach Boulevard at the end of the Pier
Manhattan Beach
310-379-8117
www.roundhousemb.com

**COST**
Free (Donations of $2 per person and $4 per family requested)

**HOURS**
Mon–Fri, 3:00 p.m.–sunset; Sat–Sun, 10:00 a.m.–sunset

**PARKING**
Varies; sometimes hard to find on summer weekends

**STROLLER ACCESS**
Good for up to a double-wide stroller, as long as you don't try to take it onto the sand

**MORE THAN ONE ADULT NEEDED?**
No

**THE LOWDOWN**
Spend the day at the beach, and get a trip to an aquarium for free.

# Santa Monica Beach/Santa Monica Pier

Santa Monica is a large white beach, and it could be a beautiful beach, but it just has too much litter and is just too crowded—at least near the pier. Move away from the pier, and it's just another L.A. beach.

The pier boasts an amusement park of the old-fashioned carnival variety, called Pacific Park. Most of the rides are aimed at teenagers, so we generally avoid them. However, a different kind of ride still lives at the pier; my kids love the beautifully restored, antique carousel that stands at the entrance, and for fifty cents a ride for kids over five, it's one of the best deals in town. The carousel horses on the outer edge do not move up and down and are perfect for kids who want to have a more moderate ride.

The pier also has miniature golf, restaurants, an arcade, and—best of all—the Bubble Man. The Bubble Man is not so much an attraction as he is a fixture; he has a cart covered in various machines that blow bubbles out into the surrounding air. As every parent knows, chasing bubbles is a great thrill for little kids, and it's beautiful to see, and all it will cost is a donation for bubble

**RATING**

**ADDRESS/PHONE/WEB SITE**
Santa Monica Pier
310-458-8900
www.santamonicapier.org

**COST**
Free entry to the pier; carousel: 50 cents for all riders over 5 years of age; unlimited ride wristbands for the amusement park: under 42 inches tall, $9.95 Mon–Fri; $10.95 weekends; over 42 inches tall, $19.95 Mon–Fri, $21.95 weekends

**PARKING**
Up to $8 depending upon time of day and season

**HOURS**
Carousel: Mon–Thu, 11:00 a.m.–5:00 p.m.; Fri–Sun, 11:00 a.m.–7:00 p.m.; closed Tue–Wed from Christmas to March 15; open 11:00 a.m.–7:00 p.m. on Christmas Day and 11:00 a.m.–9:00 p.m. on New Year's Day; Pacific Park Amusements: hours vary, call 310-260-8744

**STROLLER ACCESS**
Adequate for up to a double-wide jogger stroller; the best way to get down to the beach level is behind the carousel

**MORE THAN ONE ADULT NEEDED?**
No

**THE LOWDOWN**
Park on the pier if you can, it is easier to access than the lower lots.

soap, gas, food, rent, or whatever container you want to drop your quarters into.

Bicycles and other pedal forms of transportation can be rented at the pier as well as at nearby kiosks, and as you follow the bicycle path along you will find modern, clean playground equipment. No tickets to purchase here—clambering around on a climbing frame is free. And when you think there is nothing left to do, go to the **Santa Monica Pier Aquarium**, located under the carousel.

# Santa Monica Pier Aquarium

Under the pier in Santa Monica, this aquarium is just waiting to be discovered. The helpful staff were infinitely patient with my girls while they ran from one touch tank to the next, encouraged to feel the "gross" sea cucumbers and get "hugged" by a sea urchin.

The aquarium has a separate building that contains more exhibits, but there is enough here to keep your kids happy. They will enjoy the large fish tanks and the arts and crafts projects. In addition, one side of the aquarium is set up with a puppet show area and a book reading nook, and it's a great way to wind down after some time on the beach.

**RATING**

**ADDRESS/PHONE/WEB SITE**
1600 Ocean Front Walk
Santa Monica 90401
310-393-6149

**COST**
Children under 12, free; over 12, a suggested donation of $5 and minimum donation of $1

**PARKING**
Free

**HOURS**
Wed–Sun, 12:00–5:00 p.m.;
Tue–Fri, 2:00 p.m.–5:00 p.m.; Sat–Sun, 12:30–5:00 p.m.

**STROLLER ACCESS**
Adequate for up to a double-wide stroller

**MORE THAN ONE ADULT NEEDED?**
No

**THE LOWDOWN**
Combine this with time on the pier or the beach and you have a great outing!

## Seaside Lagoon

I wish I had found the Seaside Lagoon sooner. This is the equivalent of a heated, saltwater swimming pool with a beach surrounding it.

The Lagoon opens at the end of May and closes in September. It is a large saltwater lagoon. The water is heated by the nearby steam-generating plant and chlorinated as it enters the lagoon.

The lagoon has a couple of slides into the water as well as a children's playground. There is a restaurant and a grassy area perfect for picnics.

**RATING**

**ADDRESS/PHONE/WEB SITE**

200 Portofino Way
Redondo Beach 90277
310-318-0681

**COST**

Adults (17+), $4.50; children 2–17, $3.25; children under 2, free; annual family pass, $90

**PARKING**

$4.25 with validation

**HOURS**

Open all summer, 10:00 a.m.–5:45 p.m.

**STROLLER ACCESS**

Adequate for up to a double-wide stroller

**MORE THAN ONE ADULT NEEDED?**

No

**THE LOWDOWN**

Take a picnic and plenty of sunscreen.

## Venice Beach

Venice Beach is an experience. If you enjoy crowds of people and feeling like you have stepped back in the '60s, this is the place for you. It's reassuring to go and see people who are so strange, weird, and different that you seem pretty normal by comparison (or maybe that just works for me).

On weekends, Venice Boardwalk is covered in booths from Rose Avenue to Venice Boulevard. There is something for everyone: cheap sunglasses, socks, knick knacks, political statements. On an average weekend you will also see street performers, musicians, magicians, and art. Venice is probably the closest thing to "pure California" that you can find: reggae music, the electric guitar–playing guy on roller blades, skater kids, and Muscle Beach (a gym on the beach where men show off).

My kids and I love Venice; it's an afternoon out that costs nothing except parking, food, and whatever indispensable piece of kitsch that we can't live without that day. During the summer the sidewalk is crowded, so a double-wide stroller isn't recommended.

If the crowds become too much, move out past the bike path (which runs parallel to the sidewalk); there you will find playground equipment and—surprise, surprise—a beach.

**RATING**

**ADDRESS/PHONE/WEB SITE**
Rose Avenue to Venice Boulevard

**COST**
Free

**PARKING**
Varies, depending upon parking lot and time of day

**STROLLER ACCESS**
A single stroller will be easier to maneuver on the weekends

**MORE THAN ONE ADULT NEEDED?**
No

**THE LOWDOWN**
Go later in the day, when the sun has broken through the fog, and take sunscreen.

## Zuma Beach

Zuma Beach is arguably the best surf beach in Los Angeles or Malibu. This doesn't mean that it's a great beach for kids, and only accomplished swimmers should venture far from shore.

Zuma is, however, a large, wide, beautiful beach, which even on the busiest summer's weekend is usually not so packed that you can't find a place in the sand for your family to build sandcastles and work on a good sunburn.

Food establishments and bathrooms are far, far from the water, and it's easier to take a picnic to this beach than to try to fight your way to one of the places with hotdogs and soda. It's also really easy to tell your kids that junk food just isn't an option; they are never going to want to walk that far either.

Compared to Manhattan, Santa Monica, or most Los Angeles beaches, Zuma feels pristine and natural, and if that's what you are looking for in a beach, it's worth the drive.

**RATING**

🏖🏖🏖🏖

**COST**
Free

**PARKING**
$7 in the parking lot, although free parking may be found alongside the road

**STROLLER ACCESS**
There is no pavement or boardwalk, so leave the stroller at home

**MORE THAN ONE ADULT NEEDED?**
Yes

**THE LOWDOWN**
As at every other beach in Los Angeles, there is morning fog, so go later in the day to allow the fog to burn off.

# Southern Los Angeles

## Angels Gate Park

This park is a wonder, with possibly the best view in Los Angeles, a panorama including both the Long Beach industrial harbor as well as Catalina Island (people have always told me it was out there but, quite frankly, with the smog and haze I thought it was a myth). This park contains the Korean Friendship Bell, the **Marine Mammal Care Center, Fort MacArthur Museum,** and a summer swimming pool. Angels Gate Park is also home to two railroad clubs, which have miniature train displays in some of the buildings on-site.

The kids won't care about the enormous Friendship Bell, except as something to look at for about a minute, but this part of the park is a great place to bring a kite. There is also a playground to entertain the kids after the kite has been torn in half and tied in a knot, or they are just plain bored. It will always be windy here, so expect it (don't come on a cold winter day) and bring a coat and a kite.

**RATING**

**ADDRESS/PHONE/WEB SITE**
3601 South Gaffey Street
San Pedro 90731
310-548-7705

**COST**
Free unless you go to the museums listed elsewhere

**PARKING**
Free

**HOURS**
Open daily, 10:00 a.m.–5:00 p.m.

**STROLLER ACCESS**
Adequate for up to a double-wide stroller

**MORE THAN ONE ADULT NEEDED?**
No

**THE LOWDOWN**
This is a great city park with something for everyone.

# Aquarium of the Pacific

The Aquarium of the Pacific is the amusement park of aquariums, and as such it is both extensive *and* expensive. It features all the usual aquarium fare: touch tanks and various species of marine life—except on a much larger scale. They also have shows; the sea otters were a particular favorite of my daughter. There is also a seal performance in addition to presentations designed for kids in the Shark Lagoon, and of course feeding time is a blast.

Outside is the Lorikeet Forest, where small, friendly, brightly colored parrots will come to you to feed if you purchase nectar before you enter. I may be the only person on earth who feels this way, but the sound of a hundred happy, chirping Lorikeets is about enough to make me pull my hair out. Be warned— these things are loud, and (at least to me) hit the same pitch as fingernails on a chalkboard.

**RATING**

**ADDRESS/PHONE/WEB SITE**
100 Aquarium Way
Long Beach 90802
562-590-3100
www.aquariumofpacific.org

**COST**
Adults, $18.95; seniors (60+), $14.95; children 3–11, $10.95

**PARKING**
$6 with aquarium ticket

**HOURS**
Open everyday 9:00 a.m.–6:00 p.m., except for Christmas and the weekend of the Long Beach Grand Prix (in April)

**STROLLER ACCESS**
Adequate for up to a double-wide stroller

**MORE THAN ONE ADULT NEEDED?**
No

**THE LOWDOWN**
Take a change of clothes for the kids so they can have fun in the fountain.

Several of the exhibits are dark, particularly the jellyfish area, so if your child is scared of the dark you should probably avoid these areas. But there is also a nice area outside where they can run around and climb.

Much like an amusement park, this aquarium has too much to see, too much to do. I find myself dragging my kids and myself through exhibit after exhibit (even though we'd all like a nap) simply because we are there and the entry fee was high. So take it easy; if you don't see everything it'll be fine. The kids will love this place and you probably will too.

# Cabrillo Marine Aquarium

Cabrillo Aquarium is the aquarium you would build if you had a great love of children and sea life—and no budget. The aquarium operates on donations only. It is full of small tanks with fascinating, beautiful (and ugly) sea life. In the rear is a large touch tank that contains starfish, urchins, and other touchable sea life. There are also a couple of large tanks for watching different "fake" ecosystems, like the tropical reef and the under pier environments. The aquarium is uncrowded and fun. Many of the exhibits are hands-on and handmade, with an emphasis on education.

After you've seen the aquarium, go out to see the beach and the *real* tide pools. It's a nice day out with little ones.

**RATING**

**ADDRESS/PHONE/WEB SITE**
3720 Stephen White Drive
San Pedro 90731
310-548-7562
www.cabrilloaq.org

**COST**
Suggested donations: $5 for adults and $1 for children

**PARKING**
$7; to save the expense, take the Red Line bus (you can catch it from Ports O' Call and other places where you can park free)

**STROLLER ACCESS**
Adequate for up to a double-wide stroller

**MORE THAN ONE ADULT NEEDED?**
No

**THE LOWDOWN**
Have a fun, inexpensive trip; take a snack and use the Red Line.

# El Dorado Regional Park

El Dorado Park is so large it has been divided into three sections, El Dorado East, El Dorado West, and the El Dorado Nature Center.

The Nature Center is a great hands-on learning site, with touch tables covered in items from nature and touch drawers with animal skins and other surprises. Small creatures, from snakes to walking stick insects, surround the Center—all at child viewing height. There is a puppet theater and a comfortable rocking chair for one parent to stop and relax while watching their kids perform with the animal puppets supplied. There were only two drawbacks to the Nature Center: 1. The display of stuffed toys for sale (we escaped without buying one, but not before the witch who was working the desk yelled at me that they weren't made to play with); 2. That despite the fact that it's supposedly designed for children and accessible, the building's bathrooms don't have baby changing tables.

From the Nature Center there are three walks: a quarter-mile paved route and two unpaved routes, one or two miles. Even the unpaved trails are jogger-stroller accessible and fun. The walks are shady and would be pleasant even on a hot day; the highlight of the trail is the lakes. From the bridges we could see dozens of turtles paddling around and large fishes swimming through the murky water. There is a trail guide available for your walk at the Nature Center.

**RATING**

**ADDRESS/PHONE/WEB SITE**
East: 7550 E. Spring Street
Long Beach 90808
562-570-3100
West: 2800 N. Studebaker Road
Long Beach 90815
562-570-3225

**COST**
Free if you walk in

**PARKING**
Weekdays, $3; weekends, $5; annually, $35

**HOURS**
East: open daily, 7:00 a.m. to dusk; west: Mon–Fri, 9:00 a.m.–7:00 p.m.; Sat, 12:00–4:00 p.m.

**STROLLER ACCESS**
Adequate for up to a double-wide stroller

**MORE THAN ONE ADULT NEEDED?**
No

**THE LOWDOWN**
Just go enjoy!

The Nature Center also has family activities and special celebrations.

El Dorado East features a miniature train ride, pony rides, a petting zoo, and pedal boat rentals. And if this isn't enough, there is an archery range (the kids may have to wait for a while before they can do this), a radio controlled model plane and glider flying field, radio controlled model sailboat area, fishing lakes, and 4 miles of paved bicycle trails. Adults need a fishing license, but anyone under sixteen can try their luck without one.

El Dorado West has standard park amenities plus a skate park, which, when your kids get a little older, they may enjoy as well as playground equipment.

All in all, if you live anywhere close to this park, get a yearly pass. You will want to come again and again—it's great!

# Fort MacArthur Military Museum

Here is another treat to check out while you are in Angels Gate Park. The museum is located at Battery Osgood-Farley, which was built in 1916 and remained in active duty as an army establishment until 1974. The Battery consists of tunnels built into the hillside and the sites of the guns that once protected Los Angeles from an invasion by sea. The exhibits are mostly inside these tunnels and fortifications.

The problem is that my kids don't like the dark, and despite the lighting, this museum is dark, dank, and quite frankly a little creepy. So we just didn't get very far. If your kids are brave and unafraid of the dark, this is a nice trip, and if they are scared of the dark, climb up the hillside for a great view of Catalina.

**RATING**

**ADDRESS/PHONE/WEB SITE**
3601 South Gaffey Street
San Pedro 90731
310-548-2631
www.ftmac.org

**COST**
Requested donations: adults, $3; children, $1

**PARKING**
Free

**HOURS**
Sat–Sun, 12:00–5:00 p.m.; also by appointment

**STROLLER ACCESS**
Adequate for up to a double-wide stroller

**MORE THAN ONE ADULT NEEDED?**
No

**THE LOWDOWN**
Make a day of it and go to the other places in the park too.

# International Printing Museum

This is an incredible museum—but not a particularly great toddler museum. The small building is set up with printing presses and typography machines from various eras, and if that were all there was, it would be really dull. The joy of experiencing this museum is the demonstration of the equipment; this, however, means a tour.

The tour takes one hour—a long hour for a toddler who just wants to get up and run around and touch everything. In the tour, not only do they pour a molten metal piece of type, but they also use a replica of the Gutenberg Press to print a page of the Bible. What I am saying is, this is definitely fun to watch, but much more fun for you than for your two-year-old, who is probably con-sidering sticking her fingers in the molten metal, painting herself with the black dye, and climbing into a working printing press. You get the idea.

This is certainly one of the hidden treasures in Los Angeles; well worth the drive, the price of admission, and everything else—as long as your kids are old enough to appreciate it. I would recommend it for four-year-olds on up, but you know your kids. Just don't say I didn't warn you.

**RATING**

**ADDRESS/PHONE/WEB SITE**
315 Torrance Boulevard
Carson 90745
714-529-1832
www.printmuseum.org

**COST**
Adults, $8; seniors and children ages 5–18, $6; children under 4, free

**PARKING**
Free

**HOURS**
Sat, 10:00 a.m.–4:00 p.m.

**STROLLER ACCESS**
Adequate for a double-wide stroller

**MORE THAN ONE ADULT NEEDED?**
No

**THE LOWDOWN**
This is a must-see with older kids; if you decide not to go now, definitely go when they're a little bigger.

# Lomita Railroad Museum

I suppose I expected more than we found, but my kids were quite happy with the one large steam train, one caboose, and one tender that are inside the museum grounds. Another caboose, a water tower, oil tank car, and box car are outside the museum gates. (We found, by accident, that the museum continued across the street.) The interior of the museum features railroad spikes, (stationary) model trains, railroad documents, and other things that just couldn't have been less interesting to my toddler, so I got to study them very little.

All in all, the museum didn't justify its asking price when you consider what you can see for free at Travel Town or the Santa Fe Springs Heritage Museum. But if you are in the neighborhood, and your kids are into trains, they will have a good time. And when you've finished, there is a large, empty field where they can run until they are tired enough to fall asleep in the car.

**RATING**

**ADDRESS/PHONE/WEB SITE**
2137 West 250th Street (250th Street and Woodward Avenue)
Lomita 90717
310-326-6255
www.lomita-rr.org

**COST**
Adults, $4; children under 12, $2

**PARKING**
Free

**HOURS**
Wed–Sun, 10:00 a.m.–5:00 p.m.

**STROLLER ACCESS**
Adequate for up to a double-wide stroller

**MORE THAN ONE ADULT NEEDED?**
No

**THE LOWDOWN**
If you're in the neighborhood, go, but it's not worth a drive.

# Marine Mammal Care Center

If you follow the road through the Angels Gate park, follow the signs, ask for directions twice, and then drive around for a while, you will find the Marine Mammal Care Center. It is located right next to the Los Angeles Oiled Bird Care Center (which you can't enter). In fact, what you have come to see is in small enclosures behind the Marine Mammal building. There you will find seals and sea lions which have been injured or found ill and are being nursed back to health.

This is no aquarium exhibit with three seals that perform tricks. Instead, there are as many as forty to fifty animals of all different ages and sizes. Some have

**RATING**

**ADDRESS/PHONE/WEB SITE**
3601 S. Gaffey Street
San Pedro 90731
310-548-5677

**COST**
Free

**PARKING**
Free

**HOURS**
Open daily, 8:00 a.m.–4:00 p.m.

**STROLLER ACCESS**
Great for up to a double-wide stroller

**MORE THAN ONE ADULT NEEDED?**
No

**THE LOWDOWN**
This is a great little trip, especially when combined with the other locations at Angels Gate Park.

healing wounds, others jump in and out of the small ponds with no obvious illness. You are fairly close to the animals, but they are there for their own benefit, not for yours. The volunteers working there are more than ready to answer questions about the animals or sea mammals in general.

While I was there I ran into a grandmother with her young grandchildren. She told me they come to see the seals every day, tracking their recoveries and celebrating every time one of the animals is released back to the wild. What a wonderful activity for them to share!

Here's a place well worth a trip, and all it will cost is a donation to help feed the animals.

## Maritime Museum

Here is another short, inexpensive outing for the kids. The museum is full of miniature ships, most of them set just above kid viewing height, so you will end up parking the stroller and carrying your kid around many of the displays. In addition to models there are actual ship parts, and you may see the exacting work of model building in progress. The museum is set on two levels with a large, stroller-friendly ramp leading from one level to the next. This ramp, which features displays of dugout canoes and ships through the ages, also serves as the perfect runway for a fast-moving toddler. The staff are pleasant and relaxed and helped me catch my youngest.

**RATING**

**ADDRESS/PHONE/WEB SITE**
Berth 84, Foot of Sixth Street
San Pedro 90731
310-548-7618
www.lamaritimemuseum.org

**COST**
Donation only

**PARKING**
Free

**STROLLER ACCESS**
Good for up to a double-wide stroller

**MORE THAN ONE ADULT NEEDED?**
No

**THE LOWDOWN**
A nice little outing; it's cheap enough that if you don't love it you've lost nothing. Make sure you go outside and take a minute to watch the harbor.

Once you've seen the museum you can head out of the rear door, where there is a nice place to sit in the sun and watch the harbor. Take your kids, leave a donation, and take a quick tour. Then you can go outside to the Red Line station and take a trip to another attraction in San Pedro.

## Museum of Latin American Art

Here is one of the more kid-friendly art galleries in Los Angeles, with no guards following you around and plenty of beautiful, amazing, and eclectic pieces of art to look at. This is one of my favorite art galleries.

Art from different Latin American countries is displayed, and, for me at least, it was great to see sculptures of womanly women. There's something to be said for a culture that doesn't revere anorexia.

The gallery is currently being expanded but is open during remodeling. (I will note that they have a beautiful new restroom, but unfortunately not a changing table to be seen!) Also, they have hands-on art projects on weekends, but these are generally aimed at school-aged children and above.

RATING

ADDRESS/PHONE/WEB SITE
628 Alamitos Avenue
Long Beach 90802
562-447-1689
www.molaa.org

COST
Adults, $5; seniors, $3; children under 12, free; admission is free for everyone on Fridays

PARKING
Free

HOURS
Tue–Fri, 11:30 a.m.–7:00 p.m.; Sat, 11:00 a.m.–7:00 p.m.; Sun, 11:00 a.m.–6:00 p.m.; closed Mondays, New Year's Day, Thanksgiving, and Christmas

STROLLER ACCESS
Adequate for a double-wide stroller

MORE THAN ONE ADULT NEEDED?
No

THE LOWDOWN
This is a nice little trip, with fun artwork. If you go on a weekday you may find yourself alone in this gallery; note that the gift shop is *not* for little kids.

## Point Fermin Lighthouse and Park

This beautiful little park boasts an odd lighthouse. It looks more like Grandma's farmhouse than anyone's idea of a lighthouse. They give thirty-minute tours on Sunday afternoons from 1:00 until 4:00. Of course what I forgot was, you can't take a toddler on an architectural/historical tour. There is something about being in an empty room that makes two-year-olds want to run, and when you don't let them, they tend to scream like you're strangling them. While my youngest was cranking up the decibels, my five-year-old listened to just enough information to be worried about the person who had died in the building. After that, she apparently couldn't understand anything else that was said and made me repeat everything to her.

**RATING**

**ADDRESS/PHONE/WEB SITE**
South Gaffey Street at 807 Paseo Del Mar
San Pedro 90731
310-241-0684

**COST**
Free

**PARKING**
Free

**HOURS**
Lighthouse tours held Sun, 1:00 p.m.–4:00 p.m.; the last tour begins at 3:30 p.m.

**STROLLER ACCESS**
Good for up to a double-wide stroller

**MORE THAN ONE ADULT NEEDED?**
No

**THE LOWDOWN**
Visit the park and let the kids play, but if you want to tour the lighthouse, do it alone!

Children under forty-eight inches tall aren't allowed up the staircase to see the light, but that's fine, because you will want to drag your kids out of there before then.

## Ports O' Call Village

Ports O' Call is a shopping center disguised by cuteness. Small unique shops line the harbor, and cruises sail from many of the docks. The stores for the most part sell things like upscale china, collectibles, and in general things that probably aren't crucial for a family with small children. You can enjoy a view of the water while you eat. There is free parking, but during the weekend in the summer Ports O' Call is a zoo. After circling the parking lot for twenty minutes, I should have known better than to try to take my double-wide stroller with two hungry kids into Ports O' Call looking for lunch. There was no room to move, no room to push the stroller, and, when we finally got the food at a food court type affair (because the lines at a sit-down place were too long), we couldn't find anywhere to sit down and eat it. Ports O' Call could be entertaining, but not when it's so busy you can't move around.

**RATING**

**ADDRESS/PHONE/WEB SITE**
1100 Nagoya Way
San Pedro 90731
310-241-0684

**COST**
Free

**PARKING**
Free

**HOURS**
Open daily from 11:00 a.m.; closing times vary

**STROLLER ACCESS**
Adequate for a single stroller most of the time

**MORE THAN ONE ADULT NEEDED?**
No

**THE LOWDOWN**
If you have to circle the parking lot four times to find somewhere to park, it's too busy; go somewhere else.

# Rancho Los Alamitos

Rancho Los Alamitos is what remains of one of the last great ranchos. It contains a house, gardens, and stables with draft horses, goats, rabbits, chickens, and ducks. This should be an incredible place to take your kids; instead it rates as barely worthwhile, because you have to take an hour tour to see the house and a half hour tour to see the animals (we were allowed to see some of the gardens for ourselves, but only after my two kids had run off to play under the huge trees on the front lawn). Don't dare touch the animals, pick the flowers, or in any way upset the nice little old ladies who are keeping the Rancho as a museum.

**RATING**

**ADDRESS/PHONE/WEB SITE**
6400 Bixby Hill Road
Long Beach 90815
(Enter through the residential security gate at the intersection of Anaheim and Palo Verde)
562-431-3541

**COST**
Free

**PARKING**
Free

**HOURS**
Wed–Sun, 1:00–5:00 p.m.

**STROLLER ACCESS**
Adequate for up to a double-wide stroller everywhere except the house and the lower parts of the garden

**MORE THAN ONE ADULT NEEDED?**
Yes; you need at least two if you want to take the house tour—leave the kids in the garden with your backup

**THE LOWDOWN**
The gardens are beautiful, and if you want to just come and see them and look at (but don't touch) the animals, you will have a good time. Don't try to take the kids through the house unless they are asleep.

# RMS Queen Mary/Scorpion Submarine

The *Queen Mary* has long had a reputation as being haunted, and to cement that reputation (and perhaps to justify the $23 asking price of entry) the ship now has special effects ghosts to supplement the real ones. For a few dollars more, you can have access to the *Scorpion* submarine, a Russian Cold War–era sub; however, you can't access the sub unless you are at least forty-eight inches tall and able to climb ladders unaided. So that pretty much makes the decision for you: this is not a place to take young children. If you want to go, get a babysitter and leave the kids at home.

**RATING**

**ADDRESS/PHONE/WEB SITE**

1126 Queens Highway
Long Beach 90802
562-435-3511
www.queenmary.com

**COST**

*Queen Mary:* Adults, $23; seniors/military personnel, $20; children 5–11, $12; *Scorpion:* adults, $10; seniors/military personnel, $9; children 5–11, $9; combined ticket for both vessels: adults, $28; seniors/military personnel,$25; children 5–11, $17

**PARKING**

$8

**HOURS**

Open daily 10:00 a.m.–9:00 p.m.

**STROLLER ACCESS**

The *Queen Mary* is adequate for up to a double-wide stroller, but the *Scorpion*? You're kidding, right?

**MORE THAN ONE ADULT NEEDED?**

Yes

**THE LOWDOWN**

If you're going to spend this kind of money, go somewhere that everyone will enjoy.

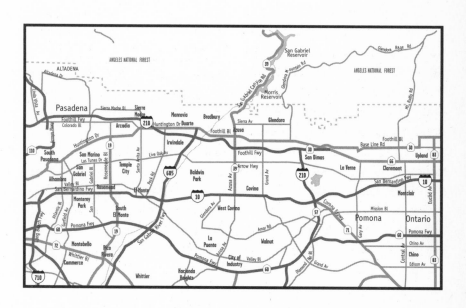

# San Gabriel Valley

# Angeles National Forest

One of Los Angeles' most notable landmarks is the San Gabriel Mountain range that rims the city to the north, yet many people never even venture into this national forest. Many Los Angeleans I know have only seen the mountains when they make the news because of fires, landslides, floods, mountain lions, or snow. This is tragic because a 650,000-acre wilderness is in our backyard, and although we will drive and spend money to go to an amusement park, we don't even motor up the hill to show nature to our children.

Make the effort; make the drive. In summer, the forest is a great place for a hike and a picnic, or fishing and camping (admittedly not for everyone, my husband included). In winter, a wonderland of potential snowballs and snow angels can be found just up the hill. Take a sled or even a cardboard box that the kids can sit on, and you can find a snowy slope amongst the pines for a day of downhill fun. In spring and fall, it's just a gorgeous escape from the city.

The forest ranges from 1,200 to 10,000 feet in elevation, with everything from sweet little walks that include waterfalls (check out Millard Canyon, which is easily accessible if you live in Pasadena) to more strenuous hikes.

The ski resort of Mountain High can be found up the 2 Highway, as can the Mount Wilson Observatory. The CHP has designated this area as

**RATING**

**ADDRESS/PHONE/WEB SITE**
Arcadia 91006
626-574-1613
www.fs.fed.us/r5/angeles

**COST**
$5, or $30 for an annual pass

**PARKING**
Free

**HOURS**
Weather dependent

**STROLLER ACCESS**
The trails vary; some are stroller-friendly, some are not

**MORE THAN ONE ADULT NEEDED?**
No

**THE LOWDOWN**
Just go, find your own personal spot, and enjoy the escape from the city.

a "daytime running lights" area, so pay attention to the signs—a ticket can be quite hefty.

A one-day adventure pass is $5, but spend $30 and you get an annual pass. This is good for anywhere in the mountains. Check that the roads are open, and take your kids on a vacation out of Los Angeles, even if it's only for a couple of hours.

# Brookside Park and Rose Bowl Aquatic Center

Brookside Park is more commonly thought of as the Rose Bowl, but it is also a large city park with all the usual amenities: picnicking areas, playgrounds, and sports play areas. There are also a few more features you should take advantage of.

The park is now home to the **Kidspace Children's Museum** and the Rose Bowl Aquatic Center.

The Aquatic Center is open year round and has two large, fifty-meter pools (one for lap swimming and one for recreation) and a smaller wading pool. The shallow end of the recreation pool is between 3½ and 5 feet deep, so it is a good depth for beginning swimmers. The center offers year-round lessons, from infants on up, although in the winter it would probably be miserable hopping out of the water into cold air. Both pools are heated (but never warm enough for me) and the kids always love it.

Also, take your kids on the three-mile Rose Bowl Loop. It's a wide paved path, and you can just look around and enjoy the beauty of the Arroyo Seco Canyon.

**RATING**

**ADDRESS/PHONE/WEB SITE**
360 North Arroyo Boulevard
Pasadena 91103
626-564-0330

**COST**
Park: free; aquatic center: adults, $2; children, $1

**PARKING**
Free

**HOURS**
Family swim hours vary; call first.

**STROLLER ACCESS**
Good for up to a double-wide stroller; most of the paths are paved.

**MORE THAN ONE ADULT NEEDED?**
Not for the park, but you need one per non-swimmer in your party for the aquatic center

**THE LOWDOWN**
On summer weekends this pool can be extremely crowded, and if they reach capacity they don't let anyone else in.

# Descanso Gardens

As soon as you get into Descanso Gardens you will have to go on the miniature train. Not only is this a great way to get a little tour of the beautiful grounds, but it is the best thing in the whole park for anyone under ten. There are some provisos, however. This minature train will not let any child under eighteen months aboard—because there are no real seats. The entire thing is a strange bench-like contraption that I would not recommend for anyone very large or with any disabilities. If you have squirmy toddlers, I recommend one adult per child so that you can hold them on the seat. When you get on the train they warn you not to wiggle, and as you go around corners the train does have a sideways sway that makes you wonder if it is going to derail—this, for my kids, only added to the excitement.

**RATING**

**ADDRESS/PHONE/WEB SITE**

1418 Descanso Drive
La Cañada 91011
818-949-4200
www.descanso.com

**COST**

General admission, $7; students and seniors, $5; children 5–12, $2; tram, $3 (trams don't run on Mondays); miniature railroad, $2 (Saturday and Sunday only)

**PARKING**

Free

**HOURS**

Open daily, 9:00 a.m.–5:00 p.m., closed Christmas

**STROLLER ACCESS**

Adequate for up to a double-wide stroller

**MORE THAN ONE ADULT NEEDED?**

No

**THE LOWDOWN**

You can't bring in food, but there is a picnic area outside.

So now that the ride portion of the day is over, there is a guided tour you can take around the grounds on a tram. For my kids, sitting for an hour and listening to a lecture about plants is the equivalent of a Novocain-free root canal, but if you think your kids (and you) would like to do it, go for it.

If you choose to walk, the grounds are not that large. When you enter you're issued a map that lists an hour and a half and a forty-five-minute walk. We finished the latter one in about an hour, allowing for the time I spent trying to keep my toddler from becoming impaled on thorns in the rose gardens. All of the main paths are large, paved road-like affairs, and even the unpaved ones were mostly accessible by jogger stroller.

The mansion on the grounds, Boddy House, reminded me of my grandmother's house, only larger and grander. My daughter couldn't grasp the concept that all four rooms downstairs were just living rooms, not bedrooms or kitchens. The house is being used as a art gallery, and as such it's far from childproof. I was eager to leave before I had to buy a shattered sculpture.

The Japanese gardens are pretty, but they lack the breathtaking beauty of **Huntington Library**'s similar garden. The Camellia Forest is probably best explored by slightly older kids who can run freely without worrying about the small, unfenced streams.

There are cheaper places to take your kids for a day of running around outside. If your kids are young enough to stay stroller-bound, you will love the beauty, and if they are a little more mobile, you will go gray attempting to keep them out of brooks and streams.

# El Monte Historical Museum and Historia Musée

Did you know that El Monte was famous for its lions? And that the MGM lion was one of theirs? We didn't either, so when we found ourselves walking through this beautiful old adobe looking at the exhibits, we kept wondering why there were lion skins on the floor. Apparently, Gay's Lion Farm at El Monte existed for almost twenty years. They bred and trained lions for movies until World War II, when it was feared that if they were bombed the lions would escape (also, meat was being rationed during the war). So all the lions were sent to different zoos, and the farm was closed.

**RATING**

**ADDRESS/PHONE/WEB SITE**
3150 Tyler Avenue
El Monte 91731
626-444-3813 or 626-580-2232

**COST**
Free

**PARKING**
Free

**HOURS**
Tue–Fri, 10:00 a.m.–4:00 p.m.; Sun, 1:00–3:00 p.m.

**STROLLER ACCESS**
Great for up to a double-wide stroller

**MORE THAN ONE ADULT NEEDED?**
No

**THE LOWDOWN**
This is a great "look don't touch" museum.

This museum is quite lovely with its tile floors and displays set up like old-fashioned businesses, schools, and houses. However, it is not necessarily set up with toddlers in mind. The only thing holding the kids back from the exhibits is a rope and signs that say "Don't Touch." Needless to say, my youngest went under the rope, ran across the back of a dead lion rug and tried to pick up a hundred-year-old baby doll from its stroller. So unless your kids have reached the age where they understand the "look don't touch" principle, or are so small they have no real options, this museum isn't for you—it's just not childproof.

Just down the road is the El Monte Historia Musée, which I am told is full of pictures and photos of the history of El Monte, but despite signs that indicated it should be open, it wasn't, and I'm not really sure I could have gotten my kids to just look at photos anyway.

# Frank G. Bonelli Park/Puddingstone Lake

Here is a beautiful manmade lake with eagles soaring overhead, herons and cranes wading at the shore, and annoying jet skis sending noise pollution all through the park. In fact, jet skiing, speedboating, and waterskiing are allowed on alternate days. In the summer, part of the lake is available for swimming and fishing is allowed (a license is needed if you're over sixteen).

There are boat rentals, jet ski rentals, horse rentals, and bike rentals available as well as a camping ground. There are many picnic areas set up for various size groups; those can be reserved in advance. However, there is almost no playground equipment.

**RATING**

**ADDRESS/PHONE/WEB SITE**
120 Via Verde Park Road
San Dimas 91773
909-599-8411

**COST**
$6 per vehicle, $3 for seniors (on weekdays); boat permit, $6 per day; rentals start at $15 per hour; horse rental, (children over 7 only) $20 per hour; pony rides (children under 7), $5

**PARKING**
Included in your admission fee to the park

**HOURS**
March 1–October 31, 6:00 a.m.–10:00 p.m.; November 1–February 28, sunrise–7:00 p.m.; closed Christmas

**STROLLER ACCESS**
Totally accessible

**MORE THAN ONE ADULT NEEDED?**
No

**THE LOWDOWN**
Here's a nice park for a hike or a picnic, if you can ignore the noisy, stinky jet skis.

## Gamble House

Gamble House is an astonishing piece of art and craft. The only way to see it, however, is by taking a one-hour, docent-guided tour. You know: that whole "don't touch, be quiet, listen to someone say things you don't understand" thing. Gamble House is beautiful: stained glass windows, various types of wood tied together with leather straps. Basically the type of beauty best enjoyed while your kids stay home.

**RATING**

**ADDRESS/PHONE/WEB SITE**

4 Westmoreland Place
Pasadena 91103
626-793-3334
www.gamblehouse.org

**COST**

Adults, $8; students and seniors, $5; children under 12, free

**PARKING**

Free

**HOURS**

Thu–Sun, 12:00–3:00 p.m.

**STROLLER ACCESS**

Not accessible

**MORE THAN ONE ADULT NEEDED?**

No

**THE LOWDOWN**

Maybe when they get a little older.

# Huntington Library

The Huntington, located in San Marino near Pasadena, is one of my favorite places. It isn't cheap to get in, but once you have entered it feels like you just left Los Angeles and stepped into a magical oasis.

The kind of wealth that built the house (which is now the main gallery) is unimaginable. Henry Edward Huntington and his wife, Arabella, took the money they had made on their railroads and put it into collecting treasures. Arabella loved English portrait paintings, and the Main Gallery is full of these works. The most famous of these are Gainsborough's *Blue Boy* and Lawrence's *Pinkie*. Henry collected books, and the library is full of treasures: a copy of the Magna Carta, a Gutenberg Bible, and more. Although none of this will have much of an impact on your kids, they'll still have a good time.

The gardens at the Huntington are great. My favorite is the Japanese Garden, where I like to just sit and think. And when we are done with that, the kids love to watch the koi swimming in the pond. My four-year-old also loves the Herb Garden. Unlike other gar-

**RATING**

**ADDRESS/PHONE/WEB SITE**
1151 Oxford Road
San Marino 91108
626-405-2100
www.huntington.org

**COST**
Adults, $12.50; seniors, $10; students, $8.50; children ages 5–11, $5; children under 5, free; admission is free on the first Thursday of every month

**PARKING**
Free

**HOURS**
Tue–Fri, 12:00–4:30 p.m.; Sat–Sun, 10:30 a.m.–4:30 p.m.; summer hours: Tue–Sun, 10:30 a.m.–4:30 p.m.; closed Mondays and most holidays

**STROLLER ACCESS**
Adequate, except in the library; a jogger stroller (single) is recommended for the gardens

**MORE THAN ONE ADULT NEEDED?**
No

**THE LOWDOWN**
Make sure it is not too hot, arrive early, and bring food with you. Eating at the restaurant is expensive and can involve a long wait on weekends. Also check to see what special events are happening. You probably won't explore the whole place in one trip, but you will want to go back again to see what you missed. Take advantage of the free Thursday because, at $12.50, this is one of the more expensive museums in Los Angeles.

dens where the plants are lovely but you had better not touch, the Herb Garden is a delight for all the senses. The plants are pretty and sweet-smelling, and if the baby grabs something and eats it, it's probably edible. The Lily Gardens and Australian Gardens are a little hike down the hill on a dirt path, but if you have a good stroller (preferably a jogger) you can navigate it. Taking the stroller through the Japanese Garden to the Zen Garden can be done, but it is difficult. Of course neither my husband nor I thought to look on the map we had been given, so, word to the wise: Before you carry the stroller up the hill with one hand while carrying the baby with the other, look at the map—there is a road.

The staff at the Huntington are helpful. When entering the main gallery with a stroller, I was approached, not to be told where I shouldn't park it, but to be conducted to the hidden elevator. On the weekend, docents are on duty. The last time I went, the docent in the Herb Garden showed my daughter herbs in their live growing and dried states.

I do not recommend going into the library with a stroller. The exhibits there are not usually of interest to toddlers, and the space is limited—particularly on weekends. If you want to bring your kids into the library, be prepared to park the stroller and carry them.

The Huntington hosts many special events. We arrived one President's Day weekend to find a re-enactment of the Battle of Lexington ongoing. It was great fun—although our baby did not appreciate the musket fire. Also, the place was packed. We actually waited an hour to buy food at the Tea House. So check what events are on before you go. And do yourself a favor—take lunch. It's a great venue for a picnic.

The Huntington closes early—at 4:30 p.m.—so get there early if you want to fully enjoy the gardens. I usually make a point of starting at a different garden each time; that way, if I get sick of walking, I still see enough. The Huntington with children is largely an outdoor venture, so pick your day; in the middle of summer go early in the morning before it gets too hot.

# Justice Brothers Racing Car Museum

This is not a spot that's easy to find. Nestled in amongst warehouses and offices, it doesn't look like a museum, and unless you are driving slowly you may not see the terrific cars inside. Here, in what is the Justice Brothers offices, they have preserved some beautiful vehicles. In building #1 (you'll see a sign to enter there first) there's a biplane hanging from the ceiling above single-seat, speed demon cars below, all shiny in chrome and bright paint. The hardest thing will be keeping your kids from wanting to touch or just jump in one; many of them look almost child-size.

A CHP motorbike and Eastern European motorcycle are also on display, and the display continues next door with 1930s Fords, more custom-built cars, and the cutest VW that looks like a one-man sub.

My five-year-old loved this place, and my two-year-old drove me crazy wanting to climb into all the cars; so judge your party and go if you can—the museum is free, and you have little to lose.

**RATING**

**ADDRESS/PHONE/WEB SITE**

2734 East Huntington Drive
Duarte 91010
626-359-9174

**COST**

Free

**PARKING**

Free

**HOURS**

Mon–Fri, 8:00 a.m.–5:00 p.m.

**STROLLER ACCESS**

Adequate for a double-wide stroller

**MORE THAN ONE ADULT NEEDED?**

No

**THE LOWDOWN**

There is a park down the street to go play at when you're through.

# Kidspace Children's Museum

After being closed for several years, the Kidspace Children's Museum has reopened in its new location in **Brookside Park**, Pasadena, down by the Rose Bowl. We managed to find it by locating the exhausted, screaming children who were being unfairly dragged away to go home.

If you live close by, you need a yearly membership here, because it's more of an amusement park than a museum; the learning is carefully hidden in a great deal of fun. After you enter through an amazing, tunnel kaleidoscope, highlights include Bug Land. In the Bug Cafe they served me insect-appropriate meals. Honestly, what kid isn't going to love giving mom or dad a "Dung Beetle Poo-Poo Platter"? There is a toddler room, but why stay there? My toddler loved climbing the leaf tower—I had to clamber after her while the five-year-old screamed, "Be careful!" at both of us.

RATING

ADDRESS/PHONE/WEB SITE
480 North Arroyo Boulevard
Pasadena 91103
626-449-9144
www.kidspacemuseum.org

COST
General admission, $8, children under 1, free; annual family membership, $100 and up

PARKING
Free

HOURS
Open daily, 9:30 a.m.–5:00 p.m.

STROLLER ACCESS
Adequate for up to a double-wide stroller

MORE THAN ONE ADULT NEEDED?
Yes

THE LOWDOWN
Bring two adults if you have more than one child, because the kids will try to run off in different directions, and there are so many things for them to do it will be more fun if you have lots of helpers.

You can also make your own earthquake (be careful on this one; it can jam young fingers—and old fingers too!), or dig for dinosaur bones, or paint watercolors on a rock wall, only to have the wall turn into a waterfall and be clean and ready to paint again. (This was a huge hit for my toddler; she got wet, and she got paint in her hair. She loved it!)

Outside you will find fountains to play in (bring a change of clothes), tricycle trails to drive on (with both large and small tricycles that seat one or two), and a garden with a rock climbing wall and a stream running through it.

On your way back inside, the kids may be tired enough to appreciate the Nature Exchange. They can bring objects they have found here, and the supervisors will help them discover what they are by looking them up in the reference materials provided. Then they can leave the item and, depending upon how rare it is, they will get points for it. The points may be used to "buy" other items, from pieces of coal to tropical shells and fossils. And if you don't have anything to exchange, or enough points, you can just come and look at all the different types of natural items they have in stock.

This museum is making a real effort to bring some fun into the city and should be supported. A great deal of thought has gone into it, and the staff are helpful and caring. They are planning to add another 60,000-square-foot building on the site, with yet more exhibits, but don't wait—go now. Your kids will love it and so will you.

# Los Angeles County Arboretum and Botanic Garden

As soon as my daughter entered the Arboretum and saw the peacocks wandering around, she declared that the L.A. Arboretum was the best place ever, and after an afternoon of wandering around the gardens and lakes she hadn't changed her mind.

The arboretum is one of those places best visited in the fall or spring, or at least in the morning, because your trip there is going to consist of walking. Although water fountains are plentiful, much of the park is not shady. The main paths are wide, paved streets, and even when you get off those into the shadier fern forest or out by the lake, most of the paths are jogger stroller accessible. Not that you'll be able to keep the kids in the stroller, because the wide expanses of grass and the wild wandering birds will tempt them to play chase or tag.

**RATING**

**ADDRESS/PHONE/WEB SITE**

301 North Baldwin Avenue
Arcadia 91007
626-821-3222
www.arboretum.org

**COST**

Adults, $7; seniors and students, $5; children ages 5–12, $4

**PARKING**

Free

**HOURS**

Open daily, 9:00 a.m.–5:00 p.m.

**STROLLER ACCESS**

Good for up to a double-wide stroller; most of the paths are paved

**MORE THAN ONE ADULT NEEDED?**

No

**THE LOWDOWN**

They don't take credit or debit cards, so take cash or a check to pay for admission. Also, the Metro Gold Line is a great way to get here, so check out www.mta.net for trains and schedules.

There is a café on the grounds and two historic houses. One, the adobe house, is fairly dull, as you can't go in. But they are working on the building so that you can look inside and see how it would have been decorated in its day. Walk through the adobe's courtyard, and you can see replicas of Indian thatched huts from an even earlier era. The second house on the grounds is a Queen Anne mansion, complete with gingerbread and oozing cuteness. If you stand across the lake and look at it, you will realize that the house looks vaguely familiar. In fact, the lake and house were seen every week in the opening sequence of *Fantasy Island*; the blue lagoon for *Fantasy Island* was this ugly, brown little pond (Baldwin Lake). The house has also been used in other productions; in fact, the last time we went it was closed for filming.

Everyone will get a good workout and have some fun. You'll remember how much walking you did and how beautiful the rose gardens were, but your kids will remember the ducks and the peacocks.

# Norton Simon Museum of Art

The Norton Simon Museum has an amazing collection of great artworks and an abundance of guards who watch your kids as if they were art thieves. This isn't a kid-oriented, hands-on museum, but at least it isn't pretending to be (like the Getty).

It doesn't get any better outside. Just look at those large stone climbing frames near the cafeteria—oh, wait, they're called sculptures, and if your toddler tries to climb one (like mine did) you will get to speak to one of the numerous guards who work there.

It's worth a visit just to see the paintings. My personal favorites are the Rembrants, but my daughter prefers Degas. You can also find works by Monet, Manet, Cezanne, Van Gogh, Picasso, and more. However, if you go with kids you had best plan a short trip, because as soon as your kids are tired of sitting in the stroller, your visit is over.

RATING

ADDRESS/PHONE/WEB SITE
411 West Colorado Boulevard
Pasadena 91105
626-449-6840
www.nortonsimon.org

COST
Adults, $8; seniors, $4.50; children under 18, free; admission is free the first Friday of every month from 6:00–9:00 p.m.

PARKING
Free

HOURS
Sat–Mon, 12:00–6:00 p.m.; closed Tuesday, Fri, 12:00–9:00 p.m.

STROLLER ACCESS
Great for up to a double-wide stroller

MORE THAN ONE ADULT NEEDED?
No

THE LOWDOWN
This is a trip that is better with either babies or kids over four.

# Pacific Asia Museum

This museum contains exquisite, ancient pottery and silk tapestries in a beautiful setting around a tranquil Zen garden. Now ask yourself if that sounds like a good place to take your kids! If you really need to take your kids to visit Ming vases, be my guest. I personally can't recommend it.

**RATING**

**ADDRESS/PHONE/WEB SITE**

46 North Los Robles Avenue
Pasadena 91101
626-449-2742
www.pacificasiamuseum.org

**COST**

Adults, $7; students and seniors, $5; admission is free every fourth Friday of the month

**PARKING**

Free in the museum's parking lot

**HOURS**

Fri, 10:00 a.m.–8:00 p.m.; Wed, Thu, Sat, Sun, 10:00–5:00 p.m.

**STROLLER ACCESS**

Fine on the ground floor for up to a double-wide stroller; there is an elevator, but once upstairs there are still steps

**MORE THAN ONE ADULT NEEDED?**

No

**THE LOWDOWN**

Go alone, or wait until the kids are older.

# Pasadena Museum of History

If you want to find the Pasadena Museum of History, follow the signs for Gamble House, and then look carefully on the other side of the street for a classy, unobtrusive sign. It's easy enough to miss, and even people who live in Pasadena have never heard of this museum—mainly because it isn't much of a museum.

The main exhibit hall is small with changing, impermanent exhibits and a shop. The museum shop is actually larger and has more to look at than the exhibit hall, which makes this an expensive but not entertaining trip.

The main part of the museum consists of two houses. The smaller of the two is a Finnish Folk Art Museum, and the larger is the Feynes Mansion. The problem is that you can't see either of these houses without going on the guided tour. An hour-and-a-half guided tour. I repeat: an hour-and-a-half, baby-screaming, toddler-chasing, kid-whining tour. The houses aren't even stroller accessible enough to take a sleeping child through. So until they are old enough to look, not touch, and old enough to listen to someone talk for an hour and a half, you can just cross this one off your schedule.

**RATING**

**ADDRESS/PHONE/WEB SITE**
470 West Walnut Avenue
Pasadena 91103
626-577-1660
www.pasadenahistory.org

**COST**
Exhibits: $5 for adults, free for children; mansion tour: $4 for adults, free for children; combined mansion and exhibit hall: $7 for adults

**PARKING**
Free

**HOURS**
Wed–Sun, 12:00–5:00 p.m.; tour times vary, so call ahead

**STROLLER ACCESS**
Inadequate—the exhibit hall is stroller-friendly, but the house tours are not designed for stroller access

**MORE THAN ONE ADULT NEEDED?**
No

**THE LOWDOWN**
Go to the Kidspace Children's Museum in Brookside Park instead.

# Raging Waters

I had wanted to go to Raging Waters ever since I saw *Bill and Ted's Excellent Adventure* in 1987, and maybe this raised unrealistic expectations . . . like that the park would be maintained and upgraded. However, this is not the case.

There are areas made just for children, specifically the Little Dipper area. The short slides in this area are made out of a soft rubber and have large, soft crash pads, but no one over forty-eight inches tall is allowed to go down the slides. So unless your children are old enough to slide alone they will not enjoy themselves. In addition, the rubber on the slides is peeling off, and the entire area needs a coat of paint. From the bathrooms with the peeling paint and original plumbing (my husband and I couldn't

**RATING**

**ADDRESS/PHONE/WEB SITE**
111 Raging Waters Dive
San Dimas 91773
909-802-2200
www.ragingwaters.com

**COST**
General admission (over 48 inches tall), $27.99; junior tickets (under 48 inches tall), $16.99 (these day tickets must be purchased online); locker rental: $4–$7; tube rental, $4–$7

**PARKING**
$7

**HOURS**
Summer only, check the Web site

**STROLLER ACCESS**
Adequate for up to a double-wide stroller.

**MORE THAN ONE ADULT NEEDED?**
Yes

**THE LOWDOWN**
Drive to Hurricane Harbor instead; don't go here with young kids.

decide if they were advanced '60s design or cheap, late-'70s design) to the peeling paint and rubber on the rides, the entire place feels seedy and dirty.

Next door, Kids Kingdom is a large climbing frame with water pouring out all over. And at the places where the handles or ropes aren't broken, kids can turn the water on and off. Hopefully it will be a very hot day, because the water in this park is ice cold. In this area too, the slide police will ensure that you don't dare slide down with your toddler, so don't try.

The whole park is quite small, so you can walk around the corner to the wave pool, which your children will not enjoy unless you rent a tube ($4 or $7 extra) for them to float on while they wait for the waves to come. This tube will also allow your young ones to circle Amazon Adventure (a river), and if they are more adventurous than my kids, they may also go on the Raging Rapids. Splash Island Adventure and Volcano Fantasea are areas where older preschoolers and parents can run around, provided, of course, your kids aren't crying that they want to go home like mine were.

In an attempt to pacify my kids we went to the food area, where we bought, for a mere $5.50, a cold, soggy piece of pizza and a small drink. We went to sit and eat it at a small tent pitched on a fake beach where we could see Splash Island. Then we saw the sign. By sitting at the "cabana" we were "reserving" it, and an attendant would be by to collect the $60 fee. Since a swarm of bees were buzzing around our soda anyway, we moved, my daughter crying the entire time and wanting to know why had I taken her to this place. I had to wonder myself.

# Ramona Museum of California History

Across the street from the San Gabriel Mission is this small museum. A variety of interesting exhibits are within, from a reconstruction of a Gabrielino-Tongva Indian hut and a replica Native American grain grinding stone that actually says, "Please Touch," to a model blacksmith setup and a sheriff's office. The central theme of the museum seems to be whether the items are interesting, and most of them are to at least one member of your party. My toddler, however, decided that the most interesting items in the museum were the antique knives displayed on the floor in the blacksmith area. After I plucked the machete from her hands, we'd pretty much seen everything.

**RATING**

**ADDRESS/PHONE/WEB SITE**
339 South Mission Avenue
San Gabriel 91776
626-288-2026

**COST**
Free

**PARKING**
Free

**HOURS**
Sat, 1:00–4:00 p.m.

**STROLLER ACCESS**
Good for up to a double-wide stroller

**MORE THAN ONE ADULT NEEDED?**
No

**THE LOWDOWN**
If you are going to the Mission on a Saturday, make a point to check this one out—just be forewarned: this museum is not childproof.

# Raymond M. Alf Museum

Located at this private school is the best museum in Los Angeles for lovers of dinosaurs. This museum was started by one of the school's teachers, Raymond Alf, and 95 percent of all the bones on display were actually acquired by the high school students and staff during field trips. Upstairs in this circular museum, your kids will ohh and ahh at the complete *Allosaurus* skeleton and the *T. Rex* skull. They'll love to pick up the items on the touch table, but it is downstairs where the fun will really start.

Make your way down the stairs (you'll have to leave your stroller behind), where the newly renovated Hall of Footprints is a pleasure. The museum has the largest collection of animal tracks in North America. It's refreshing to see casts of fossil footprints with a sign that reads "Touch." There are dinosaur noise generators the kids can try, and they can also dig for fossils or build their own dinosaur out of wooden "bones."

This is a great and surprising museum—one you and your kids will love.

**RATING**

**ADDRESS/PHONE/WEB SITE**
Located at the Webb School
1175 West Baseline Road
Claremont 91711
909-624-2798
www.alfmuseum.org

**COST**
General admission (ages 5 and up), $3; under 5, free

**PARKING**
Free

**HOURS**
Mon–Fri, 8:00 a.m.–12:00 and 1:00 p.m.–4:00 p.m.; Saturdays from September to May, 12:00–3:00 p.m.

**STROLLER ACCESS**
Inadequate—you'll have to leave your stroller on the top floor, so you may as well not bring it at all

**MORE THAN ONE ADULT NEEDED?**
No

**THE LOWDOWN**
Go!

# San Gabriel Historic Society Museum and Hayes House

This tiny little museum is great for one reason: The volunteers who are running it are so genuinely happy to have anyone come they will make you feel really welcome.

The main part of the museum has a great little doll collection as well as antique clothes; maybe it's just my girls but whenever they see vintage baby clothes they both get excited.

The house for me was like going to visit my grandma, with all the rooms set up with old furniture, toys, and the cutest antique TV. I recommend you stop here if you are going to the Mission; you'll even get to see the old jail, which looks more like a stone garden shed.

**RATING**

**ADDRESS/PHONE/WEB SITE**
546 West Broadway
San Gabriel 91776
626-308-3223

**COST**
Free

**PARKING**
Free

**HOURS**
First Saturday of the month

**STROLLER ACCESS**
Good for up to a double-wide stroller in the museum; the house is not accessible

**MORE THAN ONE ADULT NEEDED?**
No

**THE LOWDOWN**
If you are in the area on the first Saturday of the month this is a nice addition to the other San Gabriel attractions.

# San Gabriel Mission

As the fourth mission built in California, San Gabriel Mission is a great piece of living history. The church is still in use, and many of the other buildings have been reconstructed, showing that the mission was more than a church—it was a small town.

The kitchen has been recreated, and they have excavated the old tannery vats. There are large olive trees growing in the gardens, originally planted by the priests to provide olive oil for their lamps. The graveyard is the oldest in Los Angeles. In the courtyard are models of all twenty-one Californian missions as well as a fountain my children felt compelled to toss a penny into.

Besides being a great piece of history, the Mission has been enhanced by the city and made the centerpiece of the Mission District, a nice café/museum area.

**RAING**

**ADDRESS/PHONE/WEB SITE**

427 South Junipero Serra Drive
San Gabriel 91776
626-457-3048
www.sangabrielmission.org

**COST**

Adults, $5; seniors, $4; children (6–17), $3; children under 5, free

**PARKING**

Free

**HOURS**

Open daily, 9:00 a.m.–4:30 p.m.; closed holidays

**STROLLER ACCESS**

Good for up to a double-wide stroller

**MORE THAN ONE ADULT NEEDED?**

No

**THE LOWDOWN**

Make a day of it; combine this with a walking tour through San Gabriel to other sites; everyone will have a great time.

While you're in the area check out the **Ramona Museum of California History,** the **San Gabriel Historical Society Museum and Hayes House,** or **Smith Park.**

# Schabarum Regional County Park

This huge park has all the facilities you would expect and that people take for granted. As well as playgrounds, picnic areas, and room to just run, the park has a paved trail along a creek that is perfect for a stroller.

There is an equestrian center within the park, which offers horseback rides. Call them at 626-854-5560 for more details. When we last went there, rides were $20 for a half hour, but you could split the time among your children.

**RATING**

**ADDRESS/PHONE/WEB SITE**

17250 East Colima Road
Rowland Heights 91748
626- 854-5560

**COST**

Free

**PARKING**

$3 on weekends and holidays

**HOURS**

Varies by season

**STROLLER ACCESS**

Good for up to a double-wide stroller

**MORE THAN ONE ADULT NEEDED?**

No

**THE LOWDOWN**

If you live close by, this should be a favorite haunt.

## Smith Park

Just a couple of blocks from the San Gabriel Mission sits this cute park. The park has been dedicated to the Tongva-Gabrielino Native Americans and has a dry river bed and an interesting compass pointing out Los Angeles from a pre-Columbus viewpoint. But what your kids will love are the concrete marine mammals—what kid doesn't want to ride a dolphin or a sea lion? In addition the park has plenty of running room, two different play areas, and tennis courts.

**RATING**

**ADDRESS/PHONE/WEB SITE**
232 West Broadway
San Gabriel 91776

**COST**
Free

**PARKING**
Free

**HOURS**
Open daily, 7:30 a.m.–10:00 p.m.

**STROLLER ACCESS**
Good for up to a double-wide stroller

**MORE THAN ONE ADULT NEEDED?**
No

**THE LOWDOWN**
The only hard thing will be taking your kids home again.

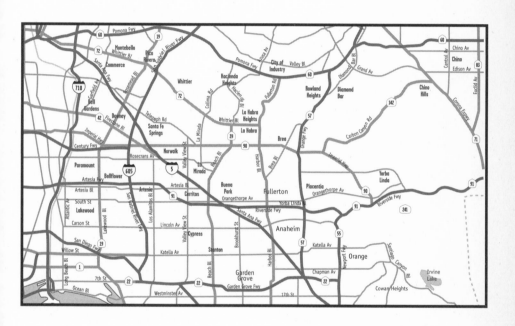

# Eastern Los Angeles

# Hacienda Heights Youth Science Center

Here, in a classroom at an elementary school, is a real surprise. This little science center may not be big or beautiful, but it's packed full of fun, educational activities for your kids. Our favorites included the live critters, a sand pendulum, an LCD display that was heat-sensitive, and electronic science games and puzzles. Your kids will love this class, and it's free. If you live nearby, go often. You'll find even more things to do and learn than we did, and your preschoolers will get the idea that school is going to be fun.

RATING

ADDRESS/PHONE/WEB SITE
Classroom #8, Wedgeworth
Elementary School
16949 Wedgeworth Drive
Hacienda Heights 91745
626-854-9825

COST
Free

PARKING
Free

HOURS
Summer: Mon–Fri, 8:00 a.m.–12:00 p.m.;
during the school year: Tue and Fri,
12:00–3:45 p.m.; Sat, 10:00 a.m.–2:00
p.m.

STROLLER ACCESS
Adequate for a double-wide stroller

MORE THAN ONE ADULT NEEDED?
No

THE LOWDOWN
Allow plenty of time—your kids won't
want to leave. They also run great
classes during the summer; call for more
details.

## Heritage Park

The city of Santa Fe Springs has really done an astonishing job creating this peaceful enclave of history. Start at the Carriage Barn (once the most expensive parking garage in Los Angeles), which is now a great little museum showing the history of the area and artifacts found on the grounds; then walk out to the garden.

Originally set up in the 1880s, the garden today retains many of the features of the original: a beautiful windmill, an English glasshouse, an aviary, and antique concrete fountains. The house is gone, but the ruins of it remain. For me, what's amazing is this park doesn't stop here. They have also recreated earlier history with

**RATING**

**ADDRESS/PHONE/WEB SITE**

12100 Mora Drive
Santa Fe Springs 90670
562-946-6476

**COST**

Free

**PARKING**

Free

**HOURS**

Park: open daily, 7:00 a.m.–7:00 p.m.;
Carriage Barn Museum and Railway
exhibit: Tue–Sun, 12:00–4:00 p.m.

**STROLLER ACCESS**

Adequate for a double-wide stroller

**MORE THAN ONE ADULT NEEDED?**

No

**THE LOWDOWN**

Do not miss out on this spot!

structures in the form of a Tongva Indian "village," including a thatched meeting house, stream, and village center.

In addition, they have unearthed the foundations of earlier adobe buildings and a trash pit and preserved them to display how archeology works: how we learn from what people throw away and leave behind. And if this isn't enough, the park also contains a railroad exhibit with a steam engine, caboose, box car, and replica station house.

This is just a great place to spend the day, and if you don't want to go home but the kids are hungry, there's a small restaurant in the center of the park.

## Montebello Barnyard Zoo

Set in a city park, this petting zoo was designed to be a gift to the community, and until recently admission was free. City kids sick of the worn-out playground equipment could go and pet a goat, see a horse, a cow, ducks, and sheep. However, due to a recent budget cut, admission is now $2 per person, and most of the kids are forced to watch the animals through the fence so their parents don't have to pay.

As with any petting zoo, don't buy food. The goats will jump anyone they even suspect has a snack, and I've never met a toddler who likes to be nibbled by a goat. All of the animals except the goats are contained within cages and corrals; the whole petting zoo is clean and rather empty.

Outside the zoo there is a hor-rifyingly old merry-go-round that looks like it should have been scrapped thirty years ago, a miniature train, and pony rides. And when you are done with all that, there is a picnic area and playground that the kids will enjoy, despite the squeaking of the rusty swing.

**RATING**

**ADDRESS/PHONE/WEB SITE**
600 Rea Drive
Montebello 90604
323-727-0269

**COST**
General admission, $2 (age 1 and over); $2 for each pony, train, or carousel ride; $1 for a bag of animal food

**PARKING**
Free

**HOURS**
Park open 7:00 a.m.–dusk; rides, Tue–Fri, 10:00 a.m.–4:00 p.m.; Sat–Sun, 10:00 a.m.–6:00 p.m.

**STROLLER ACCESS**
Adequate for up to a double-wide stroller

**MORE THAN ONE ADULT NEEDED?**
No

**THE LOWDOWN**
This trip can end up being expensive by the time your kids do everything.

154

## Pio Pico State Historic Park

I'd lived in Los Angeles for a long time without knowing who Pio Pico was, and I would probably have never found out if it weren't for this historical home. Pio Pico was the last Mexican governor of California, and his graceful adobe house has been restored and is open to the public. There is a tour, but you are also free to just explore. A twenty-minute video tells the life of Pio Pico and the history of California (my youngest actually let me watch about fifteen minutes of it before she had to explore further).

The house is partially furnished, so you can see how he lived. Also, part of the floor is open so that you can see how the excavation and restoration were done. When we walked into the parlor there was music playing. My children knew instantly what the room had been used for—they started to dance on the wooden floor.

There is also plenty of room for the kids to run around outside and have fun. Combine this with a trip to the Whittier Museum for a great day out.

**RATING**

**ADDRESS/PHONE/WEB SITE**
6003 Pioneer Boulevard
Whittier 90606
562-695-1217

**COST**
Free

**PARKING**
Free

**HOURS**
Wed–Sun, 10:00 a.m.–5:00 p.m.

**STROLLER ACCESS**
Adequate for up to a double-wide stroller

**MORE THAN ONE ADULT NEEDED?**
No

**THE LOWDOWN**
It's a nice little trip and can be combined with other local spots for a full day out. It would also make a great picnic spot.

# Workman and Temple Family Homestead Museum

You know it bodes ill for a mom with kids when you arrive for a tour and they tell you that you should go to the restroom first, because the tour is an hour-and-a-half long with no toilet facilities. After that information was delivered, I was asked if I really wanted to take my kids on the tour, because once we started there was no way out until the end. In addition, I was warned that the houses we would be entering really weren't set up for stroller access—and by the way, the kids can't touch anything.

Yeah, it didn't sound like a good idea, but I really wanted to go. The museum consists of two historic homes and a cemetery set on absolutely gorgeous grounds; but by the time we had reached

**RATING**

**ADDRESS/PHONE/WEB SITE**
15415 East Don Julian Road
City of Industry 91745
626-968-8492
www.homesteadmuseum.org

**COST**
Free

**PARKING**
Free

**HOURS**
Wed–Sun, 1:00–4:00 p.m., tours on the hour; closed major holidays

**STROLLER ACCESS**
Inadequate; historic buildings aren't the place for them

**MORE THAN ONE ADULT NEEDED?**
No

**THE LOWDOWN**
Check out the special events they hold at the museum.

the first house, my kids had had enough. The ten minutes the guide spent just telling us about the trees and the view (which no longer exists because the city has grown up around the house) was enough. I begged to be allowed to leave, and we were shown to the gate. When I'm alone, or maybe when my youngest is six, I'll try the tour again. Meantime, you can explore the El Campo Santo cemetery without a guide, and there are some exhibits to see in the gallery. The museum also hosts some special events throughout the year. Their traditional Christmas sounds like it would be fun for all, as would their summer storytelling and concert series.

# The Whittier Museum

This museum is a treasure; if you love history and want your kids to appreciate and understand it, this is the one museum they *must* visit. You step inside the large building and find yourself on a reconstructed Main Street USA. The bad news: now you need a tour. The volunteers take you through the street, through a house, past a working water pump (which kids can try), through the barn, past the model oil rig, through the Quaker Meeting House, and out to the Red Line train coming toward you.

As I've said before and as we all know, little kids do not do well on guided tours, and the guides we met (though incredibly well-meaning and helpful) cared far more than my two-year-old ever could about the details of each item and how the museum had obtained it. We were taken on even more of a tour upstairs, through more reconstructions of the past: from the family in the parlor of old to Nixon's law office. When we went past the army uniforms, I was ready to go home; my toddler had had enough thirty minutes ago. Although most everything was displayed in a practical way where nothing could be broken or touched, I was getting tired of chasing her and dragging her back to the tour guide.

Then the tour guide took us downstairs and our love for this place was not just rekindled, it was ignited. Here was a dream come true: a children's discovery center that I haven't yet seen the rival of. We were in a fully reconstructed, nineteenth-century classroom, complete with

**RATING**

🦓🦓🦓🦓🦓

**ADDRESS/PHONE/WEB SITE**

6755 Newlin Avenue
Whittier 90601
562-945-3871
www.whittiermuseum.org

**COST**

Free

**PARKING**

Free

**HOURS**

Sat–Sun, 1:00–4:00 p.m.

**STROLLER ACCESS**

Adequate for up to a double-wide stroller

**MORE THAN ONE ADULT NEEDED?**

No

**THE LOWDOWN**

Skip the tour altogether if you can, and head straight for the discovery room.

schoolbooks, slates, costumes to wear, school projects to do, and toys to play with. And we were allowed free rein to use and touch everything. When my kids got tired of playing school, they could play in a facsimile Red Line train car or with an old switchboard. The amazing thing was that we were the only people who were there on a Sunday afternoon—this place should be packed every day.

The museum runs special children's days that center around the classroom, but don't wait for that. Go now; and if your kids are getting antsy, just ask the guide if you can miss the tour of the second floor. You can catch it next time.

# Whittier Narrows Recreation Area and Nature Center

This huge 1,400-acre park has all the facilities you would expect: playground equipment, playing fields, golf course, tennis courts, and picnic areas. It also has bike rentals and equestrian trails, archery, skeet and pistol ranges, lakes (with rental boats and fishing opportunities), nature trails, and a small and aging but well-stocked Nature Center.

The Nature Center, which is located at some distance from most of the park at 100 Durfee Road, contains a variety of living animals as well as preserved examples of wildlife: raccoons, birds, etc. The highlight, however, is the live barn owl that greeted us inside the building. The Professor (as they call him) holds court over the building and is a treat to see. My oldest was astonished when we saw him turn his head until it was backwards. One of the helpful staff showed us an owl skull and explained his anatomy simply so that my kids could understand why he needed to do that.

Once you've finished in the Nature Center, it's time to take a walk through actual nature. The paths are accessible with a jogger stroller. This park is also the home of the American Heritage/Military Museum.

**RATING**

**ADDRESS/PHONE/WEB SITE**
823 Lexington-Gallatin Road
South El Monte 91733
626-575-5526
Nature Center: 100 Durfee Road
626-575-5523

**COST**
Free

**PARKING**
Free on weekdays and at the nature center, $3 on weekends

**HOURS**
Park: open daily, sunrise to sunset; nature center: Mon–Sat, 9:30 a.m.–5:00 p.m.; Sun, 11:00 a.m–5:00 p.m.

**STROLLER ACCESS**
Adequate for a double-wide stroller

**MORE THAN ONE ADULT NEEDED?**
No

**THE LOWDOWN**
This is a huge park with many entrances, so look at a map to see where you want to go.

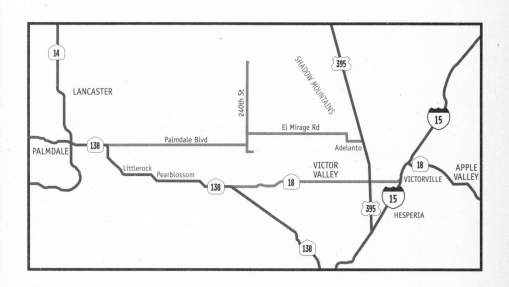

# Mojave Desert

## reeding Compound

nd yourself nearby, this is one of those amazing and rare places to visit. This facility breeds endangered cat species from around the world. Zoos from many countries send rare and endangered cats here, because the breeding program has been so successful. You can get a close-up view of some of their seventy-five inhabitants, from leopards to jaguars. Your kids, like mine, will probably think the cats are "so cute." If you are lucky, since this is a breeding facility, you may even see a cub.

The cats are only a couple of feet from you, and you need to know before you go that they are not in childproof enclosures. This makes it both easier to see them and essential that you keep your kids in the stroller, or keep a hand on them.

**RATING**

**ADDRESS/PHONE/WEB SITE**
3718 Sixtieth Street West
Rosamond 93650
661-256-3793
www.cathouse-fcc.org

**COST**
Adults, $3; children 3–18, $1

**PARKING**
Free

**HOURS**
Open every day but Wednesday, 10:00 a.m.–4:00 p.m.; closed Christmas

**STROLLER ACCESS**
Adequate for a double-wide stroller

**MORE THAN ONE ADULT NEEDED?**
No

**THE LOWDOWN**
Toddlers need to be carried or strapped down so they don't try to pet the "kitties."

It is both hot and windy in the high desert, so go when the weather is cooler, or at least later in the day, and you'll find the animals will be more active. It will only take a half hour or so to see all the animals. But I dare you to get back to your car without buying a cute stuffed toy.

# Hurricane Harbor

My first piece of advice about Hurricane Harbor is leave your double-wide stroller at home; not only won't it fit through the metal detectors, but it also won't fit through the gates at the turnstiles, leaving you to unload your children and gear and hope that someone will help you lift that stroller over the turnstiles before your three-year-old runs off. Not a fun way to start the day—and this from Six Flags, owner of more amusement parks than anyone else in America.

Castaway Cove is the perfect place for little ones. The water is only about a foot deep, and there is a small play structure in the middle. But more fun are the slides. Despite the signs saying that only one rider could ride, I was permitted by the staff to take my twenty-month-old down the slides, which both she and I loved. My five-year-old also enjoyed it, but the park designers missed one important point: crash pads. Many of the little slides have no crash pads at all,

**RATING**

**ADDRESS/PHONE/WEB SITE**
26101 Magic Mountain Parkway
Valencia 91355
661-255-4100
www.sixflags.com/parks/hurricaneharborla

**COST**
General admission, $23.99; children under 48 inches tall and seniors (55+), $16.99; raft rental, $6 or $8; locker rental, $2

**PARKING**
$9

**HOURS**
Summer only, opens in May and closes in September; check the Web site for specific times and dates

**STROLLER ACCESS**
Don't take a double-wide stroller, and don't expect stroller parking; take an umbrella stroller you can fold up and put away

**MORE THAN ONE ADULT NEEDED?**
Yes; you need one swimmer per non-swimmer in your party

**THE LOWDOWN**
Everyone should wear rubber-soled swim shoes; they will give your kids stability on the rides and help you slow down on the slides (so you don't shoot right off the end of the landing pads). Check the Web site for discount tickets.

and the bigger slides have very small ones. So I went home with less skin on my tush, and my daughter went home with less on her knees.

Also, the water in this park is cold, and I mean COLD. Do they refrigerate it? Even on a hundred-degree day it is quite a shock getting in.

Shipwreck Shores (right next door) is ideal for slightly older, more adventurous kids. It is a giant climbing frame that has water dumping on it from a giant skull. My daughters were less impressed by that than they were by the Forgotten Sea Wave Pool. This is a large wave pool and will require that you get lifejackets (provided free, both infant and child sizes available) for the kids. Also, if you really want to have fun here, a raft is vital—so plan to spend yet more money renting a single or double raft. And remember, the water is ice cold.

When I went to change the baby for the trip home, I was told that only one of the restrooms actually had a diaper-changing table. Where are the designers? I'd like to give them a thump. Yet what is best about this park is that, at least in the areas for the little kids, there are no lines. Now, it's worth going just for that.

## Kids Time Children's Museum of Antelope Valley

A strip mall is an unlikely venue for this edutainment experience. This place was one of my kids' favorites, from the fully set up hair salon, post office, and doctor's office, to the climbing mountain in the middle, and the grocery store with miniature shopping carts. The only problem was trying to keep both kids at the same activity, because there was so much to see and do.

The museum has a baby area, but if you only have babies, you don't need to be here, and if you have older kids, you will want to be playing with them—not sitting where you can't see them. On the other hand, there is a nice rocking chair for nursing the baby.

Up a narrow staircase you will find a stage and dress-up clothes,

**RATING**

**ADDRESS/PHONE/WEB SITE**
820 West Lancaster Boulevard
Lancaster 93534
661-729-1070
www.kidstime.av.org

**COST**
Adults 15 and over, $4; children 2–14, $6

**PARKING**
Free

**HOURS**
Tue–Sat, 10:00 a.m.–5:00 p.m.; closed Mondays and major holidays

**STROLLER ACCESS**
Adequate for a double-wide stroller

**MORE THAN ONE ADULT NEEDED?**
No

**THE LOWDOWN**
This would be a great place to have a birthday party.

all somewhat in need of maintenance, but my kids didn't mind that the curtains couldn't be held back properly; they were far too busy doing a show for me in the sparkly costumes they had found.

If we lived close by, I would buy a yearly membership and go on weekdays when it is less busy.

# Magic Mountain

For a park dedicated to scaring the pants off teenagers, Magic Mountain has an amazing kids' area, called Bugs Bunny World. The majority of the rides are not limited by height: My two-year-old, five-year-old, and I could all ride the same rides. The lines were small or non-existent, and there were plenty of different rides to choose from. My kids loved Pepe Le Pew's Tea Party, Tweety's Escape, and Elmer's Weather Balloons. The kid-sized roller coaster, Canyon Blaster, was too much for me and the baby, so although it goes around twice as a rule, I screamed for them to stop it after one time and they did. (I'm not much for roller coasters.)

Sylvester's Pounce and Bounce ride is limited to people whose butts will fit completely in the seats (there are some wider seats at the ends). I didn't think I was

**RATING**

**ADDRESS/PHONE/WEB SITE**
26101 Magic Mountain Parkway
Valencia 91355
661-255-4100 or 818-367-5965
www.sixflags.com/parks/magicmountain

**COST**
General admission, $47.99; children under 48 inches tall and seniors (55+), $29.99; children under 2, free (prices are regularly discounted)

**PARKING**
$9

**HOURS**
Vary; check the Web site

**STROLLER ACCESS**
Great for a single, but a double-wide stroller will not get through the ticket gate unless it is lifted over and also will not go through the metal detector

**MORE THAN ONE ADULT NEEDED?**
Yes

**THE LOWDOWN**
Check the Web site for special prices on tickets and pick a cooler day—Valencia is an oven in the summer.

that broad in the beam, but I didn't get to ride this ride. Just outside Bugs Bunny World is the Granny Grande Prix, which will give you a great view of the petting zoo. My kids loved brushing the pygmy goats with the brushes provided and watching the goose honk at us from behind the fence.

There are also shows that you can take your kids to. There is a live Looney Tunes show and an "Xtreme" bird show. The bird show consists of parrots doing strange, unnatural things like riding bikes and skate-boards. Looks like avian abuse to me, but what do I know?

Catch the huge carousel on the way out, and your day is complete. This is one of the best parks to take your kids to, and if you have some older kids along with you, they can scream themselves hoarse on the other rides and meet you at the exit.

## Vasquez Rocks Natural Area Park

This is a great place to bring the kids. If you have driven up Interstate 5, you may have seen an odd rock formation off the freeway that looks like mountains that somehow fell over. These are the Vasquez Rocks. When you get there you and your kids can either walk through desert trails, picnic in the shadow of these mighty formations, or start climbing rocks.

The rock climbs vary, and many of them are my kind of rock climbing (the kind you can do in an upright position while carrying a toddler)—more like walking up a rock path. There are even smaller rocks that were the perfect crawling-climbing size for a twenty-one-month-old and her mommy.

**RATING**

**ADDRESS/PHONE/WEB SITE**
10700 West Escondido Canyon Road
Agua Dulce 91350
661-268-0840

**COST**
Free

**PARKING**
Free

**HOURS**
8:00 a.m. to sunset

**STROLLER ACCESS**
Adequate for a double-wide stroller

**MORE THAN ONE ADULT NEEDED?**
No

**THE LOWDOWN**
Bring a picnic and lots of water. This is the high desert, so don't come on a summer day unless it is late in the evening or early in the morning.

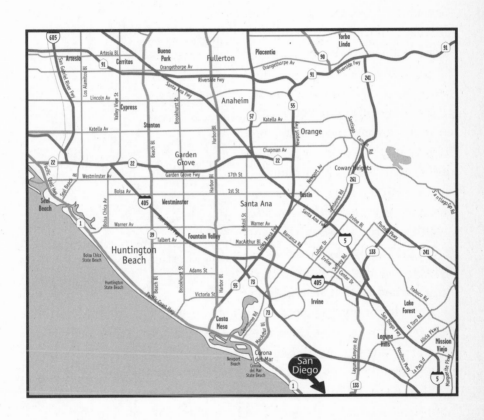

# South of L.A. County

# Adventure City

This little amusement park is the best amusement park in Los Angeles for preschool kids. It's small and lacks the magical fantasy quality of Disney, but every ride in it is suitable for young kids. Once your kids turn eight, you'll never get them to come here again, but until then, the lines are short, the rides are suitable for all ages, and you won't have to walk for miles. In three or four hours you'll have done everything and ridden more rides than you would have at one of the big parks in twelve hours.

My children's favorite was the Rescue ride, where they got to drive a fire truck. When we went to get on The Great Balloon Race, the staff member running it helpfully warned us that it might not be suitable for my youngest. Well, my two-year-old was fine on the ride, but I was terrified. Be warned—this ride goes higher and faster than other amusement park equivalents.

Relatively healthy snacks can be purchased at the park, and there are also shows. We saw two that were offered; one was great, the other, not so great, so check them out, and see what looks good to you.

Overall, if you want to take preschoolers to an amusement park, they will enjoy this one at least as much as the rest—and it will be considerably cheaper as well as easier on everyone.

**RATING**

**ADDRESS/PHONE/WEB SITE**
1238 South Beach Boulevard
Anaheim 92804
714-236-9300
www.adventurecity.com

**COST**
General admission, $12.95 (ages 1 and up); seniors, $9.95

**PARKING**
Free

**HOURS**
Varies

**STROLLER ACCESS**
Good for up to a double wide stroller

**MORE THAN ONE ADULT NEEDED?**
No

**THE LOWDOWN**
If you want to go to an amusement park with young kids, make it this one.

## Disney's California Adventure

I had heard nothing good about Disneyland's new "ugly sister," so California Adventure came as a pleasant surprise.

In fact, A Bug's Land (based on the Disney/Pixar film *A Bug's Life*) may be the best young child amusement park ever. You step into this "Land," and everything gets bigger, as you see everything from the point of view of a tiny bug. The rides are cute and imaginative, and more important, almost every one of them can be ridden by the entire family. We went on a Saturday in October, and the lines were short—five minutes or less on most rides.

One of my kids' favorite rides was Heimlich's Chew Chew Train. It's just a miniature train that goes around a small track, not much different than the trains kids could ride anywhere and shorter than most train rides, but there is a difference: the Disney touch. The magic of Disney lies in the details and creativity. On this ride you travel on a caterpillar past his favorite foods, all pretty ho-hum until you go through a slice of watermelon and watermelon-scented water drops on you. Trust Disney to find another sense to exploit; I left the ride hungry.

Near the entrance to A Bug's Land is a 3D movie called *It's Tough to Be a Bug.* There are warning signs that it may scare your kids, and you are cautioned by the staff at the entrance. When you enter you're

**RATING**

**ADDRESS/PHONE/WEB SITE**
1313 Harbor Boulevard
Anaheim 92803
714-781-4565
www.disneyland.com

**COST**
10 years and up (*yes, 10*), $53; ages 3–9, $43

**PARKING**
$9

**HOURS**
Varies, call or check the Web site

**STROLLER ACCESS**
Adequate for a double-wide stroller

**MORE THAN ONE ADULT NEEDED?**
Yes

**THE LOWDOWN**
Check the Web site for ticket specials; this is going to be an expensive outing, so I recommend enjoying it by doing the park over two days and not killing yourself trying to do it in one.

advised where the doors are in case you may have to leave. Now, this is consideration that I have not witnessed in other parks. Usually, if we have to leave, it's a problem; this time, when we left right after the show had started, we were shown out with great courtesy. Quite frankly, things popping in front of their faces isn't a good idea for little kids. If you want to see a 3D film, catch the *Muppet Vision* show at the park's Hollywood Pictures Backlot—it's funny and full of your favorite Muppets, on screen and actually in the theater.

Except for Francis's Ladybug Boogie ride, which was surprisingly rough and bumpy compared to the Mad Tea Party (the Disneyland equivalent), I found the entire area to be more fun than Toontown or Fantasyland at Disneyland: shorter lines, less walking distance, and more little-kid friendly. Oh, and did I mention shorter lines?

In addition there is a fun, live show at A Bugs Land, where your little bugs will be encouraged to get up and dance, and there is another stage in the Hollywood area where they run a twenty-minute show, "Playhouse Disney on Stage."

Another must-see in the park is the live *Aladdin* show. The show is very true to the movie, which, quite frankly, has some creepy bits, but any kid who can watch Jafar turn into a snake on TV eighteen times in a week can sit through this. It's forty minutes long, action packed, fun, and the Genie is wonderful (although your kids will wonder why you are laughing). So stand in line and go to see this one—even the most active toddler will be transfixed by the spectacle.

As you walk through the rest of the park, you can almost feel like you are traveling around California, with full Disney attention to details like the recorded birds chirping in the trees. The next fun area to take your kids into is the Redwood Creek Challenge Trail. Here they have a show based on the movie *Brother Bear,* as well as a gigantic climbing, walking, crawling play area. Some of the features, such as the rock-climbing wall, have a forty-two-inch height requirement, but there are enough other things to do to keep everyone busy.

The park is full of surprises. We ended up seeing the *Golden Dreams* movie; it was that time of the day, and I wanted just to sit.

The film was astonishingly unsentimental, and while it was still child-appropriate, it was at the same time very adult. I recommend it highly for grownups and would rate it PG for kids.

The must-see, which we missed the last time we went, is the Electric Light Parade. If you ever went to Disneyland as a kid, you probably remember how much that parade of floats and people all covered in light bulbs impressed you; believe it or not, it still wows even modern, jaded kids. The problem is, the parade isn't until just before the park closes, so it was too late at night for my mob. Before you go, check whether they are doing it at all and what time it will be. It's even worth waiting in the cold, on the cement with all the other poor suckers, because when that first float comes towards you, you'll forget how long it took to appear.

There is more to do than I have listed. The bottom line is that California Adventure may be smaller than Disneyland, and there may be fewer rides, and less everything, but your little ones will be able to do or see a lot of it. So either spread the trip over two days, taking breaks so your kids can rest and stay up late, or plan to come back again.

Also, one final note: this park is astonishingly deficient in eating establishments, and what food they do serve is, well, let me put it this way: they have a McDonald's, and that's probably the longest line in the park. So you may want to get your hands stamped and exit to Downtown Disney to find something edible.

# Disneyland

Disneyland is the happiest place on earth, for the first two hours. Then the magic starts to wear thin, your feet hurt, you've been in line for half an hour already, and your kids will start whining that they are hungry and want to see Mickey Mouse. Somehow fifteen minutes later, when Mickey finally hugs them, it will all be great again—at least until the next line, which awaits you everywhere.

Disneyland has instituted a great system to bypass the lines: it's called Fastpass. The only thing is, Fastpass doesn't work for the rides best suited to young kids, so the line for Dumbo the Flying Elephant is the longest line in the whole park. Also, pay attention to your kid; my daughter was terrified by Pirates of the Caribbean and Roger Rabbit. She started get-

**RATING**

**ADDRESS/PHONE/WEB SITE**

1313 Harbor Boulevard
Anaheim 92803
714-781-4546
www.disneyland.com

**COST**

General admission (10+), $49.75; children ages 3–9, $39.75; always check for California resident deals—one recent deal was an annual pass for $99 if you never want to go in the summer or the weekend

**PARKING**

$9

**STROLLER ACCESS**

Good for up to a double-wide stroller

**MORE THAN ONE ADULT NEEDED?**

Yes

**THE LOWDOWN**

Make a trip out of it; go for at least two days. Disneyland is best in the fall and winter, at midweek. Start your day in Mickey's Toon Town and then head to Fantasyland.

ting scared in the line for Pirates of the Caribbean, and I should have bailed at that point. It's just that I love the ride—but Pirates is scarier than you remember. If your kid is scared of the dark, avoid the Pirates of the Caribbean, and do Toad's Wild Ride before you do Roger Rabbit. Toad's Wild Ride is almost the same ride but not quite as scary. (Of course, Roger Rabbit has a Fastpass; Toad's doesn't).

Disneyland doesn't discriminate against toddlers. Adults and toddlers can enjoy rides together. Even Autotopia lets anyone over the age of one drive a car, although they won't be allowed to ride solo until they are fifty-two inches tall. And seeing people dressed up as cartoon characters is a great thrill for little ones (unless they are terrified of people in costumes—you'll find out soon enough).

The best way to see Disneyland with little kids is to take two days midweek in the fall, and stay near the park, or if you live close get a yearly pass. Disneyland is just big enough and just expensive enough that you will want to see all of it, and by the end of a long day of amusement your child will be exhausted and whining—and so will you. So realize this is going to be an expensive trip, and do it the right way: take two days or more and do the park in short bursts, allowing plenty of time for you and the kids to nap.

# Hobby City

Hobby City is an eclectic collection of hobby stores and children's entertainment. **Adventure City** is located within Hobby City, as is the Doll and Toy Museum and the Children's Living Nature Museum.

Before you enter any of the paid locations, it is fun just to walk around the stores and see model trains, planes, and houses. And when your kids tell you they want a $1,200 toy house for Christmas, you can just moan quietly. Actually, it may just be cheaper to go straight to the Doll and Toy Museum.

The Doll and Toy Museum is the large, white, antebellum-looking building. After you've paid the small fee, you can go in to look at their sizeable collection of antique dolls. If your children don't know who Shirley Temple is, then a big part of the collection will be lost on them. The good news is that the dolls are all safely behind glass, and you're left alone, so the kids can just run back and forth pointing at different things while you get your excerise following them.

The Children's Living Nature Museum is one of the other highlights of Hobby City. It contains a large collection of reptiles, amphibians, and creepy insects. Except for the weird smell that filled the room, it was great; huge snakes and scorpions are lots of fun, as long as they're behind glass.

RATING

ADDRESS/PHONE/WEB SITE
1238 South Beach Boulevard
Anaheim 92804
714-527-2323

COST
Free, except for the Doll Museum, which is $2 for adults and $1 for children

PARKING
Free

HOURS
Varies by location

STROLLER ACCESS
Good for up to a double-wide stroller

MORE THAN ONE ADULT NEEDED?
No

THE LOWDOWN
If you are down this way take a look.

# Knott's Berry Farm

Knott's Berry Farm used to be a rather quaint, pleasant place where a family grew berries, sold pies, and gave people a little thrill. The attractions consisted of a "real" ghost town of old buildings collected from around the country, a ride on a horse-drawn wagon, and an operating steam train.

This Knott's still exists, but it is buried now by a typical corporate amusement park with huge roller coasters and expensive junk food. However, if you look for it you can still find the old Knott's Berry Farm, where a real blacksmith is still hammering shoes for the horses, the steam train with a sign that says "No Spitting on the Floor" has fake robbers, and horse-drawn carriages still circle the metal terror machines (roller coasters).

**RATING**

**ADDRESS/PHONE/WEB SITE**
8039 Beach Boulevard
Buena Park 90620
714-220-5200
www.knotts.com

**COST**
Adults, $45; seniors, $35; children 3–11, $14.95

**PARKING**
$9

**HOURS**
Varies, call or check the Web site

**STROLLER ACCESS**
Great for up to a double-wide stroller

**MORE THAN ONE ADULT NEEDED?**
Yes

**THE LOWDOWN**
There are still picnic grounds available outside the park; take a picnic lunch and save some cash.

Knott's has one feature that I haven't seen in other amusement parks: each ride has a thrill rating, and the ratings from 1 to 5 are fairly accurate. Preschoolers can easily handle any 1 or 2, and more adventurous young souls can probably handle a 3. The 4 and 5 rides are usually height restricted above forty-eight inches, and even if they aren't, they're not kid rides.

Camp Snoopy is the kids' area, and it suffers from too many rides which are limited to kids over thirty-six inches tall. This means you can't take your two-year-old on rides that she could ride at a Disney amusement park. There are also a couple of kids' rides where you must be less than fifty-two inches tall, so you can't ride with your kid. All in all, there are few rides a family with mixed-age children can actually enjoy. Camp Snoopy has a stage show, which is entertaining but far from wonderful; but at least it is one of the few things everyone can do. Also, some of the more scream-inducing roller-coasters actually travel overhead in Camp Snoopy. This upset my kids—it's hard to explain that the people are screaming because they are having a good time.

Outside of Camp Snoopy there are some fun things you can do as a family, most notably, the shows. The Wild West Show features gunshots and fighting—too many gunshots for my girls, but your kids may feel differently. They also have Indian Dances in this area. There is a great show in the Calico Saloon; take your kids in, buy a sarsaparilla, and watch a family show with Can-Can girls (my great-great-grandmother is probably rolling in her grave). There is also an Indian mystic show at the Mystery Lodge.

The ghost town area of Knott's is actually great for kids, except in October. Make sure to find the 1880s schoolroom; your kids will love sitting in the tiny desks, and there is a "schoolmaster" all dressed up and ready to answer questions. Then, of course, there's the wagon ride and train ride.

But don't go in October, because the park is dressed up for "Halloween Haunt." I made the mistake of going on October 1, when mummies were hanging from buildings as decorations and there was actually a large skeleton holding a dismembered leg. Camp Snoopy is decorated in a kid-friendly way, but you won't want to spend the whole day there.

# Movieland Wax Museum

This newer, larger, less run-down museum is nonetheless run by the same people who own the Hollywood Wax Museum. Here you can roll your children through an intricate maze of lifeless figures set in dark theatrical lighting, in poses from movies that neither you nor your child have ever seen.

If the dark lighting and glass-eyed stillness doesn't scare your kids, some of the sets (like *The Poseidon Adventure*) may, although you can avoid the Chamber of Horrors. When you finally find a character they know, that may interest them. However, if they are anything like my kids or the other kids I saw in the museum, their first response will be, "But that doesn't look like so-and-so."

There are so many great places in Orange County to take kids; this just isn't one of them.

**RATING**

**ADDRESS/PHONE/WEB SITE**
7711 Beach Boulevard
Buena Park
714-522-1155
www.movielandwaxmuseum.com

**COST**
Adults (12 and up), $12.95; children (4–11), $6.95; seniors (55+), $10.55

**PARKING**
Free

**HOURS**
Mon–Fri, 10:00 a.m.–7:30 p.m.; Sat–Sun, 9:00 a.m.–8:30 p.m.

**STROLLER ACCESS**
Good for up to a double-wide stroller

**MORE THAN ONE ADULT NEEDED?**
No

**THE LOWDOWN**
Go to Adventure City instead.

# Legoland

After visiting Legoland I developed a new pet peeve: amusement parks that charge you for activities within the park. I realize this isn't a new trend (and may have even been the norm back in the day), but the degree to which my kids *only* wanted to do the things that cost extra money in Legoland was just ridiculous. Especially when the park excludes young kids from just about everything and then puts "Dig Those Dinos" on the top of their list of what to do with your two-year-old, and it's one of those pay-as-you-play options.

My-five-year-old had a great time at Legoland. Why? Because she's over forty-two inches tall. Basically Legoland works like this; if your kids are all over forty-two inches, this park will be great fun. If almost everyone is thirty-six inches or more, this park will be good. If anyone in your party is under thirty-six inches, they will be bored or just plain mad, and so will the poor sucker who has to hold them while their big sister or brother gets to do everything. There are at least two rides that are identical to Disneyland rides: Flight Squadron (like the Dumbo the Flying Elephant ride) and Bioni-

**RATING**

If all kids are over thirty-six inches

If all kids are under thirty-six inches (stick to Explore Village)

If you have mixed-size children

**ADDRESS/PHONE/WEB SITE**

1 Legoland Drive
Carlsbad 92008
760-918-5346
www.legoland.com

**COST**

Adults, $43.95; children 3–12 and seniors (60+), $36.95; children under 2, free

**PARKING**

$7

**HOURS**

Closed most non-summer Tuesdays and Wednesdays, open 10:00 a.m.–5:00 p.m. most other days; extended hours during the summer; check the Web site or call for current hours

**STROLLER ACCESS**

Adequate for up to a double-wide stroller

**MORE THAN ONE ADULT NEEDED?**

Yes

**THE LOWDOWN**

If you really want to do an amusement park with mixed-age kids, go to a Disney park instead.

cle Blaster (like the Mad Tea Party teacup ride). The difference is, at Disneyland my baby would have squealed in delight on the rides, but at Legoland she had a tantrum over not being allowed on them.

If you are going to Legoland, take my advice and take kids who are all the same height. That way either *no one* can ride the rides, or *everyone* can. If the kids' heights vary, be prepared to split up your party.

Also, consider yourself warned: If you have one or more Lego aficionados in your group, it's going to be very difficult to get out of the park without spending big bucks on souvenir Lego sets!

At least the shows are fun. The Big Test show not only reinforced fire safety, but actually entertained everyone, including the grandparents. Highlights for us ended up being the oversized playstructure called Hideaways; the Explore Village, which is really an area with glorified park equipment; Miniland USA, the Lego small-scale model world (actually quite spectacular); and Fairy Tale Brook, which is a better version of Disneyland's Storybook ride. On the whole, Legoland, with its long lines and unreasonable height requests, only served to make me really appreciate how great Disneyland is.

# San Diego Wild Animal Park

Kids and animals—now there's a combination that really can't go wrong. This zoo without cages is one of the best animal breeding facilities in the world, and personally I prefer this setting to feeling sorry for the poor animals doing time behind bars.

Most of the animals are visited by taking the one-hour tram ride around the park. Because of the nature of the park, this can sometimes be less satisfying for the young ones than a regular zoo. When you go to see the lions you may not find them in their enclosure, and the animals don't just walk up to the train. They are out there, but sometimes only binoculars will really let you see the details.

The park does its best, how-

**RATING**

**ADDRESS/PHONE/WEB SITE**
15500 San Pasqual Valley Road
Escondido 92027
760-747-8702

**COST**
Adults, $28.50; children 3–11, $17.50

**PARKING**
$8 for non-members, $6 for members

**HOURS**
Open summer 7:30 a.m.–8:00 p.m.; winter 9:00 a.m.–5:00 p.m.

**STROLLER ACCESS**
Adequate for up to a double-wide stroller

**MORE THAN ONE ADULT NEEDED?**
Yes

**THE LOWDOWN**
Check the Web site for cheaper tickets; you can also get a discount if you buy combined tickets to both the San Diego Zoo and the Wild Animal Park.

ever, to give the visitor as well as the animals a great experience, and the little ones will love the Petting Kraal and the shows. Our favorite was the elephant show, with the bird show a close second. My kids also loved the Lorikeet Landing, where they got to feed a $2 cup of sugar water to pretty little parrots.

Like most amusement parks, by the end of the day this one will be too much. You'll be exhausted; you'll have walked forever, and your kids will need a nap. So if you can, split your visit over two days or, better yet, if you live close-by, get a yearly membership, and do the park in many short trips.

# APPENDIX
## My Prejudiced Guide to Strollers

In my humble opinion, there are only two kinds of strollers worth owning: a jogger stroller and a small umbrella stroller. I love my jogger stroller. I own a double-wide, and both of my kids like riding in it. I make it a point not to jog, but a good jogger stroller is easier to push than a regular stroller, and the large wheels make it easy to roll over most terrain. (I'm still seeking a completely all-terrain stroller that will roll fully loaded over soft sand, but my stroller does great on most other surfaces.) It's worth the money—buy one good jogger stroller, and get rid of the one with the tiny wheels.

The only other kind of stroller to have is a small umbrella stroller. This is the one you can fold up easily, store behind the seat at a show, or carry with ease up and down stairs. There are places where you will carry the stroller as much as push it—and the less it weighs, the better, obviously. This being said, I would still recommend an umbrella stroller with a pouch on the back (in which you can put a bottle of water and some diapers) as well as a sun shade.

Before you take that pretty stroller home, test drive it. Push it around the store. If the handles aren't at the right height for you, or you can't fold it up to get it in the back of the car, forget it and keep shopping!

# General Index

# Category Index